D1477802

Values That Shape Us

Inspirational Stories and Quotes

by

Manjulika Koshal

DORRANCE PUBLISHING CO
EST. 1920
PITTSBURGH, PENNSYLVANIA 15238

The contents of this work, including, but not limited to, the accuracy of events, people, and places depicted; opinions expressed; permission to use previously published materials included; and any advice given or actions advocated are solely the responsibility of the author, who assumes all liability for said work and indemnifies the publisher against any claims stemming from publication of the work.

All Rights Reserved
Copyright © 2022 by Manjulika Koshal

No part of this book may be reproduced or transmitted, downloaded, distributed, reverse engineered, or stored in or introduced into any information storage and retrieval system, in any form or by any means, including photocopying and recording, whether electronic or mechanical, now known or hereinafter invented without permission in writing from the publisher.

Dorrance Publishing Co
585 Alpha Drive
Suite 103
Pittsburgh, PA 15238
Visit our website at *www.dorrancebookstore.com*

ISBN: 978-1-6386-7316-3
eISBN: 978-1-6386-7664-5

Values
That
Shape Us

Inspirational Stories and Quotes

by

Manjulika Koshal

This book is dedicated to my parents,
Inderjeet and Satyawati Badhwar,
the source of my inspirations.

Table of Contents

Foreword

Values are the most essential part of our lives, the core of who we are. We form our set of values from the institutions to which we are connected: our family, schools, religion, occupation, and society. Like the air we breathe, our values are often taken for granted and not apparent to us until we are asked about them. Then we are forced to examine them and nudged to articulate them. The author of this book has given us precisely that opportunity.

This book has been put together by the author in a unique way. The first section is a collection of personal stories written by people known to her. Each contributor was given the freedom and space to write about values that shaped their lives, the values they live by, and what gives them joy. The stories do not preach, nor do they proport to be a directive for life. They are engaging incidents and snippets of life that have profound meaning to the writers. Our author does not discriminate nor judge but accepts everyone's contribution as valid and important.

The second section of the book is a selection of stories that appeared in media, collected by the author, showing the fearlessness of various men and women from different walks of life. Most have had difficult family lives, often coming from dysfunctional families, facing poverty and sometimes abuse. Yet, in their personality is a certain strength and, in the stories, some hidden values through which they have faced and overcome these adversities. The author highlights and profiles several women who she feels have had even more challenges in life than men, and yet succeeded.

In the final section of the book, the author shares what she has been inspired by: things she has read, short stories and quotes, as well as messages that came to her via social media or stories narrated to her by colleagues, friends, and family. These are little reminders of the beauty and complexity of life, and the need to be positive and courageous.

In writing the foreword to this book, I have reflected upon my own values and the early events in my life when I was uncertain about how to reach my potential. My parents did not agree that I should attend college, given the expense and the distance from home. However, my employer encouraged me to pursue my goal of becoming a physical therapist and enrolling at the University. I was inspired to trust myself and not let others deter me from taking the risk, despite the financial obstacles I would face.

In my life, Rotary International—a world-wide service club—is an institution that has been an inspiration to me and thousands of others, working to make the world a better place. I was privileged to know and to be mentored by my friend Dr. Atmaram Gawande, who was the president of our local Rotary Club and later the district governor. He was a model for a life based on Rotary's motto of "Service Above Self," and he inspired me to experience the joys of giving. My involvement with Rotary has been a long one. I have served as president for two separate terms and have held several positions on the Board of Directors for over 20 years.

Inspiration is invaluable to a successful life and comes to us in many ways. Sometimes people inspire us; at other times, various customs, and norms; and sometimes the wonders of nature and our planetary system. For example, in the solar system, all parts work together in perfect harmony every day, reminding us of the value of doing our duty truthfully and systematically, in compliance with society's codes of conduct.

Alfred Lord Tennyson, inspired by the river, wrote the well- known poem, *The Brook,* and the famous stanza, "Men may come, and men may go, but I go on forever." The poem is a tribute to obstacles a river faces but keeps moving.

Sometimes, our value systems and universal codes of conduct inspire us to be disciplined and we imbibe these values, which in turn shape our thinking, our personality, and our course of life. The values conveyed through life experiences, stories and quotes in this book are universally accepted by society. They shape, change, reform, and reconstruct our thinking, personality, habits, norms, and behaviour, enabling us to become truly evolved individuals.

Since we have only one life to experience, we can benefit by hearing the stories of others' lives, the lessons they learned, what inspired them. It's an opportunity to reflect on our lives and give thanks and gratitude for the moments that give us satisfaction or joy. For those of us who have struggled, as most of us have, it's a chance to celebrate the victories and face the future with hope and faith.

This book has a unique appeal and will be an asset for all, serving as an effective tool of encouragement, inspiration, and learning.

Sheila Mark
President, Athens Rotary Club (2020-21)
Athens, Ohio, U.S.A.

Acknowledgements

It is hard to write acknowledgements in any context, but it is harder when there are so many persons who have helped to bring my vision of the book to fruition.

I would like to acknowledge my colleagues and friends, near and far, who inspired me and supported my idea of putting such a book together.

I am grateful and indebted to Ms. Sheila Mark, who graciously agreed to write the Foreword for the book. Sheila has been a fellow Rotarian and friend for 24 years. In her long career as physical therapist, she experienced how values transform humans and influence their rehabilitation.

Anita Anand, my cousin, urged me to realize my vision, making suggestions on its content and structure and editing the manuscript. Working with her has been an educational process, as I learned to incorporate ideas, merge thoughts, and more importantly, what to leave out. She has efficiently assisted with reframing of ideas and interweaving them. Till the very end, Anita has been with me in every step of the process, encouraging me. I thank her for her patience.

Mahesh Uppal assisted with the technical layout of the manuscript.

Members of my family—my husband, children, and grandchildren have motivated me. Rajindar Koshal, my husband went over the entire manuscript, taking care of all the technical details. My special thanks to him.

The G.K. Vale Studio in Bangalore, India, improved the image of my parents' picture for the dedication page of the book. In two days, they did the job and e-mailed it back to me. I am thankful to them for their prompt service and a job well done.

Dorrance Publishers, especially their Senior Consultant, Mr. Adam Johnson, helped by explaining the nitty-gritty of submitting the manuscript.

Putting a book together has its technological challenges, especially for me. My son Vipin and grandson Adeel helped with the intricacies of the computer, both with software and hardware. Adeel, a freshman at Vanderbilt University, assisted in formatting pages of the book and also contributed a story to Part I of the book. My daughter, daughter-in-law, and other grandchildren helped in many ways.

The stories in Part I are written and shared by people known and connected to me—my housekeeper in India, office support staff, medical staff, friends I have known for a long time in India—whose parents were colleagues of my parents; other family members, including my cousins, especially on my husband's side, a 95-year-old-plus uncle. To all, my heartfelt thanks.

Family, colleagues, and friends living in the United States gave inputs to the book. Students, administrators, and others associated with Ohio University at Athens, Ohio, where I worked, made suggestions and contributed their personal life experiences. Whomsoever I talked to about the idea of the book, supported it.

I feel blessed to be surrounded by loving people and am grateful for their inputs and suggestions. Each of my six grandchildren listened carefully to stories embedded in family values I learned from my parents and grandparents, which I passed on to their parents, and their parents are passing on to them. This was my incentive to begin and complete the book. Finally, my local friends, Indian and American, in my town, Athens, Ohio, gave suggestions, and some contributed to the book.

I could go on forever. However, I will say that it is not possible to write such a book without inspiration, encouragement, and support of family, friends, relatives, academic colleagues, and students. I am indebted to all and grateful for their help. I am especially indebted to those who wrote their stories of real-life experiences.

Introduction

This book was inspired by an incident in my personal life.

Some years ago, I visited a close friend who was seriously ill and had to quit working. On one of my visits to him, I presented him a book of quotes *Life's Instructions for Wisdom, Success and Happiness* by H. Jackson Brown Jr. I thought the book would cheer him up.

Ten days before his death he returned the book to me, saying, "This book was a great source of inspiration for me and kept me going. It healed by mind and body. Thank you."

I asked if he would like to share some valuable facets of his life, about how he became a doctor. He said he would be happy to, sharing that when he was young, one of his close relatives was extremely sick, and he was upset about it. He was told that the town they lived in had no specialist to treat this person. That day, according to our friend, he decided that no matter what it took, he was going to become a doctor. The town he lived in had no medical school. So, he moved to the closest city that had one and eventually became a doctor. The rest is history.

His determination and perseverance in overcoming the numerous obstacles on his journey enabled him to achieve his goal. He suggested to me that if one could write a book of stories conveying inspirational values, it would be very healing to those who were sick and/or had given up on their lives.

I thought about what my doctor friend had said and began asking people if they had such stories to share. Over a period, I realized I had enough material to put together as a book. Besides these personal stories, I have been inspired by reportage in media about people overcoming life's adversities and emerging successful and confident. So, I added some of these to the book.

As inspirational quotes appeal to me, I thought about supporting the stories with quotes. Hence this book.

About the Book
The book is about values and how people have overcome their life circumstances by perseverance, hard work, determination, and faith in themselves and others around them.

The book has three parts. Part I has personal stories by contributors who are known to me. Part II consists of true stories or anecdotes collected in my research. Part III are quotes on the same themes as Part I and II.

It is not a scholarly book, nor is it a self-help one. I have listened to what people have told me, asked them to write their stories in their own words, and done some research myself. The references you will find are not scholarly either, but informal, as that is how the book is intended.

It is meant to inspire, lift the spirits, and serve as food for reflection.

Who Will the Book Appeal To?
I hope the book will appeal to a wide spectrum of people of all ages. Young people might like to read stories of values that shaped their parents and grandparents. Older people might be curious about the experiences of other elders. And for those who are unwell, distressed, and suffering, I hope it will be a source of healing, and inspiration for living with hope.

What Are Values?
The term "value" has broad connotation. It is used widely in various disciplines, references, and contexts. The word value comes from the Latin word "valere," which means "be strong, be well, be of value, be worth." Value is defined as the worth, usefulness, or *importance of someone or something*. For example, this person or thing is important or beneficial in some way; in other words, valued.

According to this definition, it can be said that the "importance of someone or something" may vary widely. It may be subjective. However, there are some concepts, ideals, or codes devised by human beings over the ages that are "universal." Examples can be the Ethical Codes of Conduct or the Statistical Standards of Measurement. These codes or standards are universally accepted, used, and practiced.

Values in Various Disciplines
In Economics, value is defined as the relative worth or importance of a product and is generally measured by assigning a monetary weight or currency, such as dollars, pounds, or the currency of the country in reference. This measurement would be called the "economic value or worth" of an item. Economic value is the measure of the benefit from a good or service to an economic agent. It is typically measured in units of currency. Another interpretation is, "it represents the maximum amount of money an agent is willing and able to pay for a good or service."

In business, finance, or accounting, generally the economic worth or value of the product or stock is used for determining value. However, in business and other organizations, there is another facet of the term "value" or "core values" that are the driving force for setting standards.

Core values are universal and present in various kinds of organizations, such as business, societies, religious, political institutions, legal, scientific, educational, and medical institutions. Each institution has its "Code of Conduct" embedded in their Mission Statement and are the principles that guide its behavior in business and beyond.

For example, Smarp, the employment communications platform, in their blog say: the core values support the company's vision and shape its culture. It is the only way you can build "trust" in the workplace.

Values in Society

In societies, core values dictate behavior and determine the difference between right and wrong. They are influenced by religious or ethical norms that constitute a universal code of conduct. These norms are recognized in all societies. Some examples are not to steal or lie, not to harm others, and work faithfully, diligently, and honestly. The norms build trust and faith in one's dealings with others. Many religions also have these norms in their teachings.

Another definition of these norms is "human values," which influence human behavior, attitudes, and personality. Over a period, people form their beliefs and attitudes, and thus each person is different. Social values reflect how we relate to society and include justice, freedom, respect, community, and responsibility.

This is the reason I wanted to write such a book, where contributors, through their personal stories, convey social values.

In layperson's terms, we understand human values as teachings that are handed down by our elders and ancestors, for generations. According to Miriam Webster dictionary, the first time the word "value" was used was in the fourteenth century, and "there are a couple of ways to define value as a noun. First off, it is the amount of money that something is worth, or its price. Secondly, it is something that can be bought for a low or fair price. Value is based on its usefulness or importance. In other contexts, it is used as relative worth, merit or importance. Example, the value of a college education."

There are other ways that the term values are used. In philosophy and religion, "values are standards or ideals with which we evaluate actions, people, things, or situations. Beauty, honesty, justice, peace, and generosity are all examples of values. Values drive our actions, and they motivate goals. The goals help to set our priorities in life, guide our decision-making, and affect our evaluation of our success and happiness in life.

Values form the foundation of our lives. They influence our behavior and actions. As such, values can be reflected in various ways—as quotes, stories, commandments, or actual experiences.

The Origin of Values

Values are not born or created. They are unconsciously learned or evolve over a period from our environment—family and home, school, work, and society. In families, the values imparted come in many forms, as behavior and teaching by elders and rituals and customs. Examples could be being respectful to all, especially elders; greeting all who visit your home with an open heart and generosity; and being kind to the deprived, less privileged, or have-nots. These are some examples of values we imbibe from our home unconsciously. More details on these values are in the table provided at the end of this section.

How Values Benefit Individuals

Good values learned over years enable the making of a good citizen, a person who is kind and generous and can be trusted.

Differences Between Values, Trust, Beliefs, Faith, and Habits

The above concepts are linked to each other. Values obtained from various environments influence us unconsciously, forming a set of beliefs that further influence our attitudes towards life. In the long run, all the above concepts together mold and frame personalities and habits. Other traits, such as ambition, self-confidence, hope, and determination can evolve during life's journey. This relationship is shown in the table below.

It is difficult to figure out the source of the value or trait. Is it the home, outside the home, work, friends, inspiration from the lives of others, reading of literature, or what? Sometimes, the difference between trust and belief are hard to separate. A short story I received from a friend, illustrates the fine distinction between the two concepts.

A juggler was performing a trick by walking on a wire tied between two solid concrete poles. His young son was on his shoulders while he balanced himself with the support of a long stick. The crowd was watching with suspense. All were tense. When the juggler reached the end of the pole, the crowd cheered and clapped. The juggler then asked the crowd if they thought he could walk back on the wire from where he started. The crowd confirmed with confidence his question and emboldened him. He asked the crowd if they trusted him. There was a loud roar and overwhelming support. The juggler then asked the crowd, "If you trust me, would any of you come forward and sit on my shoulder just as my son did?" He assured the crowd that he would take that person carefully and safely. There was a complete silence in the crowd.

This story shows the difference between trust and belief. The crowd believed that he could retrace his steps back to the first pole, but they did not trust that he would be able to carry one of them on his back.

Belief is an acceptance that a statement is true or that something exists. It is something that one accepts as true or real, a firmly held opinion or conviction. Trust, on the other hand, means a firm belief in the reliability, truth, ability, or strength of someone or something.

In the story of the juggler, the crowd accepted the ability of the juggler in walking back to the first pole. But when it came to trusting him over carrying one of them, there was doubt. The trust was missing. Belief is the product of the mind while trust is the product of both mind and heart. When you are believing, it is just like you are expecting to earn something; but if you are trusting, you are totally surrendering all of yourself no matter what the outcome is—for better or for worse.

Faith, on the other hand, has no reason or evidence. The American professional bowler Don Carter says, "Faith is believing something to be real or true or will be real or true in future without any evidence. Faith may provide comfort but not truth."

Hope, on the other hand, is open ended, without any expectation. For example, I hope I win the lottery. Faith is hope plus expectation. Faith is the substance of hope.

Trust is based on evidence. Author and columnist Nolan Dalla says, "Trust is based on evidence, what is real according to human reason and it is the core conviction of judgment based on knowledge, instinct and experience."

Habits and faith are the result of our attitudes and beliefs. For example: I believe in this religion; I have faith, and so I go to church on Sundays. That becomes a habit.

The stories in this book cover all the above ways in which values play themselves out in our lives. From the time we are born and become aware of the world around us, till the time we die, we are imbibing values. Values define us and make us the persons we are. Without values, we would be lost and be adrift.

The context of this book

This book centers around human and ethical values that are the core of human behavior. The stories reflect the values learned in one's personal life from family, institutions, the environment, and other influences which help to shape attitudes and personalities.

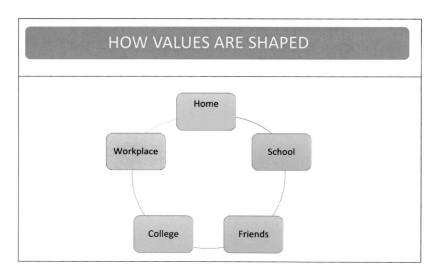

HOW VALUES ARE SHAPED

Home

School

Workplace

College

Friends

THE HOME ENVIRONMENT

Friends of Parents	Respect for Institutions	Teachings, Stories, Experiences, Rules of the House
Festivals, Social Gatherings	Doing your Best, Generosity	Faith in the Almighty

LEARNED VALUES

Welcome guests & friends with an open heart	Aim High and Work Hard	Be Determined

Repect for all, especially the elderly and poor	House is Open to All

VALUES GET INGRAINED

- Personality types are formed and these become habits.

RESULTS

- A good citizen emerges, with the *values* of hope, trust, faith, love and duty.

Part One
First Person Stories

Introduction to Part One

This section of the book is a collection of first-person inspirational stories of experiences of the contributors.

The stories are about human and ethical values, such as love, compassion, hard work, dedication, sacrifice, discipline, happiness, depression, encouragement, kindness, battling rigid customs, living in poverty and overcoming it.

The stories highlight faith, trust, belief, and hope and valuable lessons the contributors learned. The contributors are students, professors, administrators, doctors, engineers, homemakers, friends, and relatives. They emphasize the value of living a truthful life and bearing witness to inequality, injustice and discrimination and working to eradicate it.

Each of the stories are unique and different, experiences that had a profound impact on the lives of the contributors and were instrumental in changing their outlook on life, their personality, behavior, and attitude.

Story 1

From Fear
to Confidence and Self-Determination

By Manjulika Koshal

Growing up in India, my family and I lived in Dhanbad, in the state of Bihar (Dhanbad now is in the state of Jharkhand). My father was the Deputy Chief Inspector of Mines in the Government of India. Today, Dhanbad is the second most populated city in Jharkhand, referred to as the "Coal Capital of India."

During the 1950s in Dhanbad, there were no colleges, except the prestigious Indian School of Mines (ISM), specializing in Mining and Geology. Today, it has grown and is a technical institution with 18 departments and part of the well-known chain of the Indian Institutes of Technology (IIT).

In 1955, when I was ready for college, 10 other young women, daughters of mining engineers from the Dhanbad area, and I were enrolled at the Patna Women's College in Patna, 165 miles from Dhanbad. It was run by nuns of the Order of Sisters of the Apostolic Carmel and was a reputed institution.

Travelling to and from college by train, a staff person accompanied us. One night, my father, or Papa as we called him, told my mother, Mummy: "From now on, Manju" (this is my nickname by which I am addressed by most of my family and friends) "must travel by herself with the other women." It was an overnight train, and we had reservations in the ladies' compartment. My mother was really upset. Finally, he said, "Either Manju goes alone, or it is over for her."

Papa persuaded other parents, too, to join him in this decision. We were all scared of traveling alone, and none of us slept that night. Reaching Patna, we had to take a cab and tell the driver how to get to the college, which we had never done before. Reaching the college, we all heaved a sigh of relief, feeling like we had climbed Mount Everest!

Overnight, I became fearless. It changed my life. There was a feeling of a winner. This experience has helped me in building a "mind set" by which I could face any hurdle in life with confidence and self-determination. And to this day, I thank my father for this. Anytime I face a dilemma, it reminds me of this incident and my dear Papa.

Story 2

How Values Are Transferred to Children

By Manjulika Koshal

In Athens, Ohio, our home is always open to guests or anyone who comes—a mailman, a house cleaner, a helper for the yard, or others.

My husband and I have tried to be gracious hosts. Perhaps we conveyed this indirectly or unconsciously (thinking back) to our children to never fret or get angry if unexpected guests walk in. One can always come up with ideas how to fix more and be hospitable and share food and drink smilingly.

For Vipin, our son's graduation from Chapel Hill, North Carolina, five of us travelled for the commencement. Vipin shared an apartment with two other friends, whose relatives were also coming. It was supposed to be a total of 12-15 guests. Vipin planned the menu and assigned tasks to everyone. He bought and marinated 20 pounds of chicken in yogurt sauce to barbeque *tandoori chicken*. A day before the graduation, many additional guests started visiting them. Vipin's friends panicked and were angry that they were not informed about these additional numbers.

My son, calm as ever, said to them, "What's the big deal? The sky has not fallen, and we will manage."

He went to the store and bought more Naans (Indian readymade breads), cut vegetables, pies, and ice-cream. We all helped in the cooking. It was a lot of fun.

At the end of the evening while relaxing with beers, his friends asked, "Vipin, we are amazed that you never got nervous or angry. How come?"

He replied, "I learned this from my mom and dad, who always entertained and greeted guests and students with open arms, any time of the day."

It made me think about how values get passed on in families, indirectly or directly, contributing to personality development.

Story 3

The Importance of Treating Everyone with Respect, Including Your Parents

By Manjulika Koshal

A. My husband and I, every now and then, visit the O'Bleness Hospital in Athens, Ohio, our hometown. Our family name, "Koshal," rings a bell with the medical staff who ask if we are related to our son Vipin, who practices at the hospital.

Invariably, they say, "He is a doctor without a chip on his shoulder. Often, at lunch time he joins the nurses' table in the hospital cafeteria and dines with us. He has a profound love for humanity."

What a powerful lesson for all of us.

B. My father, when he left home for work in the morning and returned in the evening, touched his father's (my grandfather's) feet, who lived with us. In India, touching someone's feet signifies deep respect. In Hindu temples, devotees pay respect to the Gods by touching their feet or prostrating before them. I recall the respect my father had for my grandfather, who raised him well—to become an educated, successful, and respected human being. My grandfather, who had little education and came from a modest background, raised my father alone as he lost his wife early in the marriage. But my father did well, excelling in school and getting scholarships. He got a full scholarship to the well-known Indian School of Mines at Dhanbad. In India as is in other cultures, a deep respect for your parents and elders in the family is taught in the home, from childhood.

Story 4
The Value of Good Ethics

By R. D. Malhotra

This is a story about my granduncle, who is 92 years old. When he was about 10 years old, he and his family lived in a small village in the state of Punjab, where everyone knew each other. It was a small community and like a family.

One afternoon, his father gave my granduncle money and asked him to go to the store and buy some sugar. The store was half a mile away. My uncle went to the store, and while the shopkeeper went inside to prepare the order (in those days, the groceries were not pre-packaged but stored in gunny bags in large quantities), my uncle noticed a jar full of chocolates. He could not resist them and helped himself to three chocolates. The shopkeeper may have noticed the chocolates in my granduncle's hand but did not say anything to him. My granduncle brought the sugar home.

At home, his father asked him if he had the sugar. My granduncle nodded his head and said, "Yes."

His father noticed the chocolates and asked, "Did you buy those also?"

My granduncle started crying and told him that he had helped himself. His father was angry and said, "What does not belong to you is not yours. And since you did not buy the chocolates, they are not yours. Go back right now and return the chocolates." It was sunset and getting dark, and his mother was worried that he would get lost getting back. But my granduncle's father insisted.

As my granduncle tells the story, he went all the way back in the dark, afraid he would lose his way. Still, my granduncle, with courage, walked alone in the dark, frightened but determined to return the chocolates and get back.

The shopkeeper was amazed that such a young boy was told to return what did not belong to him. My granduncle apologized to the storekeeper, and as he was about to return, the storekeeper said, "Wait a minute, dear child, here is a handful of chocolates for you as a reward for your truthfulness, honesty, and admitting your fault."

But granduncle refused to take the chocolates, fearing that he might be scolded again by his father. Although this time, the chocolates were a gift, his father may assume that he had stolen them. He remembered what his father had said, "If it does not belong to you, it is not yours." My grand uncle remembers this incident till today, and according to him, it made a profound influence on his life, career and personality.

The story shows that it's incorrect to take what is not rightfully yours. When narrating this story, he says he is not lured by precious things that belong to others.

Today, he is a successful, well-settled, rich, but humble businessman with great ideals.

Story 5

The Value of Challenging Traditions

By Manjulika Koshal

My maternal grandfather, Mr. Mehar Chand Puri, was the Chief Station Master in the Indian Railways in the town of Batala in the North Indian state of Punjab. He was also a freedom fighter, participating in Mahatma Gandhi's "Quit India Movement," a demand to end the British Rule of India in the early 1940s.

My mother was one of three daughters and a son. In the 1930s, she and her sisters attended the Kanya Maha Vidyalaya, or literally, the "Great Women's College" in the town of Jallandhar, Punjab. At the Kanya Maha Vidyalaya, the medium of instruction was Hindi. My grandfather deliberately sent them to this college as he strongly believed that they should not use anything "British," but "Indian" or "Swadeshi" (of one's country) to support the nationwide movement promoting Indian-made goods and a boycott of British made goods. So, my mother, aunts, and uncle got their higher education in well-known Sanskrit schools and colleges.

My grandfather knew that English, as a language, was not a part of the curriculum at the Kanya Maha Vidyalaya. So, he hired an English teacher to tutor my mother and aunts as he realized the value of English as a language of communication with the world. The teacher came to the college and tutored my mother and aunts after their college classes.

The college also offered music classes, such as sitar, harmonium, violin, and singing. My mother and aunts also studied these. After their graduation, my grandfather employed for them music tutors at home for advanced music and singing classes. My grandfathers' relatives and friends used to frown and say, "Puri Sahib" (his last name was Puri) "you are preparing your daughters to be dancers in brothels." In those times, it was unusual for young women not only to study but also learn to sing and play musical instruments.

All the music training paid off for my mother in later life. She was a great singer and gave violin performances at the Rotary Club meetings (I watched her play) where my father was the president.

My grandfather showed courage in standing up to society and fighting conservative thinking. He was a liberal and a democrat and believed that women should be well educated and well versed in learning skills they might need in their lives. As a result, he encouraged all his children to aspire for higher education, to be bold and stand up to traditions that stood in the way of their progress and development.

Story 6

The Inspiration to Learn

By Ravi Badhwar

When I was six or seven years old, my father, who I called Papa, was teaching me how to count to 100. At that time, I could count to 10 or 20. When Papa came home from office, he would sit down with me, and we would practice my counting. I was making little progress, and when I became a father, I realized it is not easy to learn to count at that age as memory isn't fully developed. So, I would count to 15 and then go back to 7 or 8.

One day, Papa came home from office and settled down. He asked me to bring my counting tablet, which held rows of large plastic beads loosely tied together with a wire, so they can be moved as one counts. I tried my best to focus and not lose track on the continued stream, but when I reached 40, I had to backtrack again.

Papa was very frustrated. So, he went to his bedroom and brought a box with shining gold coins in bundles in fine brown wrapping paper. I was so excited at seeing the coins, thinking I had counted very well, and Papa was rewarding me.

However, as we sat down, Papa said, "Kiki" (what I was fondly called at home) "listen, I am going to give you two hours to learn all your counting from 1 to 100, without making any mistakes. No jumping ahead or going backwards when counting because you lose your sequence. So, practice, and I will test you after two hours. I will give you two chances. If you mess up the first time, you will be given one more chance. If you can correctly count all the way from 1 to 100, this jar of coins will be yours."

This was a real challenge to me. I started dancing at the idea of this reward and began to earnestly learn my counting, practicing all the time with the counting slate, jumping all over the house. I must have sounded funny. I practiced by rote, so I would remember. I went to everyone in the house—my mother, my siblings, and the house staff—asking them to listen to my counting. It was a vigorous exercise for those two hours.

Two hours later, I still remember, I started counting. When I reached 80, Papa held up the coins, and said firmly: Now remember this is your last chance. I don't know what happened, but I remember that I knew I could not make a mistake. And, before I knew it, I had counted to 100 with my eyes closed. Papa said: "Kiki stop, you did it, you passed."

I started dancing with delight and Papa gave me the coins.

From this experience, I learned that it's important to inspire a learner and give an incentive. Papa's promise of a jar of coins was my incentive. I also learned that it is important to focus and make an effort. I am a religious person and have faith. I feel the Goddess of education, Saraswati, and the goddess of wealth, Lakshmi, guided me.

Story 7

The Value of Friendship

By Satish Dewan

Growing up in the 1950s in the city of Calcutta, India, I have happy and fond memories of my father, Mr. H.R. Dewan, and his three friends who stayed with us, in our three-bedroom apartment on Chowringhee Road.

My father was the Director of the Indian Bureau of Mines and posted in Calcutta, in the state of West Bengal. Mr. Grewal was Chief Inspector of Mines, and Mr. Jabbi and Mr. Inderjeet Badhwar were deputy chief inspectors of mines and needed to come to Calcutta for meetings.

We were a family of several children, so mattresses would be put down in our living room floor to accommodate guests.

My father and his friends would spread out on the mattresses and chat well past midnight. I can remember and still hear their laughter, happiness, and joy as they joked and talked. My father's friends were in the same profession as his, working in India's mining industry. They were all graduates of the first batch of the well-known Indian School of Mines at Dhanbad (then in Bihar and now in Jharkhand) and close friends.

While all three visiting friends could well afford to stay in the best of hotels, they wanted to be together, even if it meant to sleep on the floor. This was a true friendship.

There is a proverb in Hindi, "Rishte tab bhi the, rishte abh bhi hain." This means, "We were connected before and are connected even now."

Story 8
Awareness of Cultural Values and Their Importance

By Saroj Sawhney

My two sisters and I grew up in West Bengal in India. My father, whom we called Papa, was the manager of several coal mines in an area called Chinakuri. We sisters went to school in Loreto Convent in Asansol, the town about 12 kilometers from Chinakuri.

The school was run by the Sisters of Loreto, a Catholic missionary group originally from Ireland and devoted to education of girls. The school was exceptionally good as the Catholic nuns and teachers were very dedicated. I adored the nuns, and they made a deep impression on me. I started going to the school chapel every day. It was a calm and attractive place with great spiritual aura and good energy. While I never fully understood the Catholic faith, I liked the rituals and bought rosaries (a necklace with beads and a cross), like my Catholic classmates.

My parents and grandfather (on my mother's side), whom we called Pitaji noticed this. Pitaji told my father: "These children will become Christians." He suggested we attend a Hindi-medium school to learn our values and culture.

My father replied, "Pitaji, please suggest some ways, so the girls learn about our culture."

This conversation led to the start of a ritual known as "havan," which involved recitation of prayers around a fire, with offerings of ghee (clarified butter), and air purifiers every Sunday morning at home. Pitaji was ecstatic. We learned to recite the havan mantras or shlokas, and to this date, I remember them. Pitaji was a staunch Arya Samaji, a member of a breakaway group of mainstream Hinduism, which did not believe in deities, but rather the belief that God is omnipresent and everywhere, and one does not need to go to a temple to worship.

I am blessed to have such parents and a grandfather for inculcating such values in us. Our father was a brilliant mining engineer and an upright person. During his career, many subordinates brought money or gifts in return for favors. My father politely refused these and asked them to use it for their families.

I am happy and proud to say that my husband Jasbir, myself, our daughter Nomita, and Abhishek, our son-in-law, all share the same values today.

Story 9

Value of
Determination, Empathy, and Love for Family

By Rajen and Nipun Luv

It was the wedding of our youngest daughter in Bangalore, India, and we were happily busy with the preparations. Almost all the arrangements had been finalized for a great Punjabi wedding. Our eldest daughter, who lived in Chicago, and our second daughter, from Singapore, were with us, too.

One day, late in the evening, our eldest daughter suddenly felt unwell and had a seizure. We called an ambulance and took her to hospital. We were there all night as the hospital ran tests. An MRI indicated that she had a brain tumor and that, too, was at an advanced stage. The attending doctors advised immediate surgery, as a delay was risky.

We discussed postponing the wedding, but our eldest daughter insisted that we continue as planned, so her younger sister could start her new life in Seattle, U.S.A.. We held the wedding the next day, and after it, she flew back to Chicago, undergoing major surgery for the very advanced stage of brain tumor around the optic nerve, diagnosed as GBM Grade IV.

From this event, I learned that values are not necessarily transferred from parents to children. In our family, our children have been role models to us in learning empathy for family members, love for siblings, and an extraordinary strong will to face a tough situation.

Story 10

The Power of a Positive Attitude

By Cyndi Parsons

I am a great advocate of the saying "laughter is the best medicine." I have tried to live every day with a happy spirit, trying not to worry until absolutely necessary, being kind to everyone I encounter, and seeing the good in everyone. Just a simple smile to someone can change their day.

I recall a rare stop I made one summer day for a McDonald's iced coffee, whipped cream and chocolate drizzle on top, before I went to work. Walking through the parking lot, a man in a white truck was waiting on his co-worker to come out. He, too, had an iced coffee he was drinking. We looked and smiled at each other.

I said, "You know it's going to be a good start of the day," as I held my iced coffee in a "cheers" fashion.

He held his up out the window and said, "You bet."

We smiled again at each other, and I walked on into the building.

I thought how nice it was to smile at someone, exchange friendly words, and start the day off with a good feeling. Then I thought how easy it was to be positive and how sad it was that people chose to be negative. Even when I feel a little down or "off," I react positively because in the end it brings me back up.

Story 11

The Value of Caring and Appreciating Each Other

By Pramilla Rajan

A math teacher asked her students to do an assignment: to list the names of each student in the room on two sheets of paper, leaving a space between each name. She asked them to think of the nicest thing about that person and write it down.

Over the weekend, the teacher wrote down the name of each student on a separate sheet of paper and listed what everyone else had said about that person. On Monday, she gave each student the lists she had compiled. Before long, the entire class was smiling.

"Really?" she heard whispered. "I never knew that I meant anything to anyone!"

And "I didn't know others liked me so much," many said.

The assignment was not mentioned in class again. The teacher did not know if the students discussed their lists after class or with their parents. It did not matter. The exercise had accomplished its purpose. The students were happy with themselves and one another. That group of students moved on.

Several years later, one of the students was killed during the war at the India-Pakistan border in Kargil. The teacher attended the funeral, her first of a serviceman. The place was filled with his friends.

As she stood there, one of the soldiers who acted as pallbearer came up to her.

"Were you Sanjay's math teacher?" he asked. She nodded: Yes. "Sanjay talked about you a lot," he said.

After the funeral Sanjay's former classmates as well as his parents came to speak to the teacher.

"We want to show you something," his father said, taking a wallet out of his pocket. "They found this on Sanjay when he was killed. We thought you might recognize it."

Opening the wallet, he carefully removed two worn pieces of notebook paper that had been taped, folded, and refolded many times. The teacher recognized the paper on which the students, in their class assignment, had written about Sanjay's good points.

"Thank you so much for doing that," Sanjay's mother said. "As you can see, Sanjay treasured it."

Sanjay's classmates gathered around.

Arjun smiled rather sheepishly and said, "I still have my list. It's in the top drawer of my desk at home."

Prithviraj's wife said, "My husband asked me to put his in our wedding album."

"I have mine, too," Rashmi said. "It's in my diary."

Deepali, another classmate, reached into her pocketbook, took out her wallet, and showed her worn and frazzled list to the group.

"I carry this with me at all times." he said, and without batting an eyelid, continued, "I think we all saved our lists."

The teacher was so touched, she broke down and cried. She cried for Sanjay and for his friends who would never see him again.

This story shows how easy it is to focus on the good points of each other, take time to think about them, and share it with them. It is a form of caring and appreciating the other. Often, we tend to think of the negative aspects of other's personalities.

It doesn't take much to focus on the positive.

Story 12
Memories of Values

By Kathleen Marinelli

My mother lived through the Depression. She told me how her brothers jumped onto trains, to steal and toss coal to those waiting so that they did not freeze to death.

Valuing education and respect for teachers, I was expected not to get into trouble at school and was told, "If you get in trouble at school, it will be worse for you at home."

Further, I was instilled with the idea to make sure that my children had a good education.

Then, there were lessons for life such as, "Always wear clean underwear—you never know if you will be in an accident!" And, that I did not need to copy others: "Just because someone jumps off a bridge, doesn't mean you must also!"

My grandparents prayed every day, and I learned about the importance of faith. Sundays were spent at the homes of my grandparents, which taught me the importance of family.

Story 13

Lessongs from Curiosity

By Kelly Shears

When I was five years old, I was curious about my grandfather's beer. He was sipping his beer and happened to put the can on ground near his rocking chair. I got curious. I thought, *I wonder how the beer tastes?*

So, while my grandfather was absorbed reading his paper, I tiptoed and sneakily picked up the beer can and took a few gulps. It was bitter, and I did not really like the taste. A little later, I threw up.

My grandfather laughed after realizing what happened.

He said, "Good for you, Kelly. It is a great lesson for you never to touch alcohol. In the long run, it will keep you sober."

Till this day, I don't drink beer, and I can instantly smell it on someone who has had it.

This story conveys an important message that sometimes you learn valuable lessons in life only through experience and curiosity.

Story 14

The Value of Kindness

By Katie Boehlefeld

The greatest lesson I have learned is to always be kind to everyone.

My mother has taught me this through her loving attitude and caring heart. She is a nurse at Akron Children's hospital in the state of Ohio, U.S.A. When I was younger, my sister and I would go with her to work events at the hospital. The first event I remember was the "Kids Are Number One Run," and our task was to help her work a table at the race. This is when I saw my mother interact with her patients and people in the community. Most of them were children who were either injured or extremely sick. They were going through a tough time and seemed incredibly sad.

My mother was not affected by this and went right up to them. She had them play games and get their faces painted. I saw them open up and begin to smile. It was utterly amazing.

My mother taught me that it is important to be kind to people, even if they are not open to it at first. I have adapted this in my everyday life and strive to give everyone I can, a smile. It can be as simple as holding the door for someone or giving someone a compliment. We never truly know what someone is going through, so it is so important to BE KIND.

Story 15

Value of Faith, Perseverance, Strong Family Ties, and Positive Thinking

By Rajen and Nipun Luv

Values are learned by observing or listening to life experiences of people in families.

We would like to share a narrative from our parents talking about those terrible days of the partition of our country after British rule in 1947. Like many families, our parents also suffered, and we want to share the values we learnt from them, such as positive thinking, faith, strong family ties, and perseverance.

Before independence, our parents and grandparents were settled on the other side of the border, which later became Pakistan.

Rajen's mother was pregnant when she had to suddenly leave home with her in-laws to look for new life on the Indian side of the border. Rajen's father was posted in another city, and he had no clue where his pregnant wife and his parents had gone. After many tense days, they established contact with his father, who was supposed to take a refugee train to India. When the train arrived, all passengers had been massacred along the way. Fortunately, Rajen's father had not boarded the crowded train and arrived much later in a well-guarded train.

Meanwhile, Rajen was born in the middle of turmoil and great uncertainty. It was the strong beliefs of grandparents and sheer willpower of his father to see his first new-born child which later united the family.

We learned the values of being hopeful, positive, perseverance, faith, and building strong family ties.

Story 16

The Value of Good Relationships and Respect

By Rajindar Koshal

A. LOOKING FOR THE GOOD IN RELATIONSHIPS

My parents taught me that nobody is perfect, and everyone has some imperfections. So, I was taught to look for the good qualities and ignore the imperfections or bad qualities, especially of relatives and close friends.

This advice helped me to have extra close relationships with my relatives and friends. At many weddings when I have been asked to give blessings to the newlyweds and I say: "Nobody is perfect; so, for a successful marriage, look for each other's good qualities and ignore the not so good ones."

I myself have followed this principle all my life. As a result, I have close and sincere relatives and friends.

B. RESPECT OTHERS AND YOU WILL BE RESPECTED

In 1942, I was living in the town of Kasur in the state of Punjab, India, which is now in Pakistan. My father was principal of the Hindu high school. His school helper (known as "peon" in India) belonged to the lowest rank of the Hindu Caste ladder, known as untouchables.

I was 10 years old. On a Sunday morning, my father wanted the school helper to do some schoolwork. At that time, telephones were almost nonexistent, so my father sent me to this person's home to give his message. His home was about half a mile away from ours. I walked over and knocked on the door and was greeted by his wife. She invited me in, and I saw that the home was quite basic—it was a one room house without running water. The couple were newly married and had some sweets left over from their wedding day. They offered me the sweets. At first, I was reluctant, as I had heard that one should not take or eat anything—leave alone touch—from an untouchable person. But I thought over and realized that their feelings might be hurt if I refused. I therefore took the sweets, knowing it would make the couple happy.

I gave my father's message and returned home. I told my father that his message was delivered and told my parents that the helper and his wife offered me some sweets from their wedding day, and I ate them. My parents told me that I did the right thing by accepting the sweets, as it must have given great pleasure to the newly wedded couple.

I know that any other family would not have approved of my action, but on the other hand, they would have reprimanded their son or daughter.

In my life, I try to treat people with respect. In Bangalore, my wife and I have a winter home, where we spend three months every year. Often, our staff have told us that when they visit our home for any repair, etc., they get tea and other goodies and so much respect, which is not the case with other villa owners. The majority of the owners, treat plumbers or any helpers as mere workers and not human beings.

Story 17

The Value of "Lombardi Time"

By Steve Clusman

Growing up in Green Bay, Wisconsin, I learned the value of being prompt and on time, no matter what the occasion, through the notion of "Lombardi Time."

"Lombardi Time" is a principle that comes from Vince Lombardi, legendary former hall of fame coach of the Green Bay Packers. Lombardi instilled in his team a simple rule: If you didn't show up 15 minutes early for a meeting, you were considered late.

He won many championships and brought the first ever Super Bowl championship to the small town of Green Bay, Wisconsin. The entire town cherishes the history of this team and specifically the legendary status of Coach Lombardi.

Growing up, this value was instilled in me by my family, my peers, and my coaches. It was easy for me to buy into this mantra because I was a diehard fan of the team and was highly involved with athletics throughout my entire life. I can recall my father saying on multiple occasions, "Are you going to be on time? Or are you going to be on Lombardi Time? Because if you are just on time, you are already late."

I believe this way of thinking really helped me develop from a young athlete to a professional in the workplace. It has shown me the importance of being prepared and showing respect to others. I try to hold myself to a higher standard, because I find value in what it brings to me and also what it may bring to others.

I viewed promptness and being early as a sign of respect and showing others that you care. Regardless of how others perceive the act of being early or late, I wanted to make a good impression.

I think back to this classic saying when preparing for many events. I respect time and wish to respect those who I interact with on a daily basis. I hope to carry on this tradition and spread the message of "Lombardi Time" and other values to those who I meet along my journey. It connects me to my family, my hometown, and to others.

Story 18

The Value of Simplicity in Life

By Manjulika Koshal

When I was growing up at home, we did "havan" every Sunday. A havan is a ritual among Hindus where offerings are made, and mantras chanted around a small fire in a four-cornered iron vessel called a "havan kund." After havan, there would be discourses to guide us through life.

My mother's older sister, whom we called Chopra auntie, and her two daughters were living with us. Chopra auntie became a widow suddenly and early in her marriage. While she was trying to get re-settled, my father invited her to stay with us and be an older sister to him since he did not have a sister.

One day, during "havan," there was an incident. Pitaji (my maternal grandfather) and his wife who used to also live with us noticed that Chopra auntie's older daughter Hem, whom we called Hem Didi, had grown her nails, filed them, and used nail polish.

He said to me: "Manjulika, go and get a pair of scissors." I was perplexed as to why he needed the scissors at that time.

Pitaji took the scissors and Hem Didi's hand and started cutting her nails. I can still remember tears rolling down Didi's cheeks. But neither she nor anyone present had the guts to say anything or stop Pitaji. He then said: "Khabardar" (beware) "in future I do not want to see any of these things related to fashion."

Pitaji believed that fashion and dressing up, etc., distracted the young mind away from studies. He then lectured all of us young people as to why at this stage in our life the main goal was to focus on and excel in studies, have high ambitions, and settle down with a brilliant career. Only then, we should focus on other material things in life. And there was a lifetime to be into fashion, clothes, and jewelry.

What a lesson of simplicity for living a full life!

Story 19

Value of Effort and Keeping Connections

By Morgan Glenn-Simons

As I sit here and think about "values" I hold true to my life and the way I live, I see that many things matter to me, but they can be combined into a few words: time, connection, and effort. These are the three words I take into consideration when making any decision and therefore are the qualities I value most.

I have always valued the time I spend on anything, whether it be time with family, with friends, studying, or anything else. My parents split when I was an infant, and I have had to divide my time with them equally over holidays, summers, and weekends. This was simple when I was young, but with age, I had extracurricular events and friends who I wanted to spend time with. I learned at a young age that it is not just the quantity of time that matters, but the quality of that time spent.

Branching off having good quality time, I found that in order to have success in limited time, I had to build strong connections with those who I was spending time with. Each and every family member and friend I have, I feel we bond on a level that is so hard to reach for some. Seldom did I ever sit around and do nothing; I would always want to be up and doing something because I found that doing something with others helps build relationships and make them stronger.

In order to maintain such strong relationships, I learned that effort must be apparent. I know that the people who try and put forth effort, or show they want to be with me, or show they want to help me are the ones I am closest with. The bond with them is stronger than with others, because of the effort put in by two, that is me and them. Alongside effort in relationships, effort I put into my schoolwork and my jobs has paid off equally as well.

These three values I hold true to myself and the way I live are actively reflected now. I became aware and learned these three things when I was young, but I consider them my values for the simple fact that I apply all three to my daily life. As a college student who holds three jobs, volunteers weekly, and is in good academic standing, I have to manage my time wisely and carefully. I have noticed connecting with people, such as students, coworkers, and professors has made such an impact on my college career. The ability to rely on them, to have trust in them, and have them feel that way about me is remarkable.

Lastly, I see the effort I put in making a change. I recently got accepted into a master's program and can thank my efforts in academics. I can also attribute my acceptance to the effort I put in at all my jobs and the hospital I volunteer at because they have given me such good experience.

Story 20

The Value of Values

By Sharmila Jayasuriya

I grew up in Sri Lanka with my parents and my two siblings. From a young age, my parents imparted to us the value of education. My mother was a high school teacher. My father started his career as a schoolteacher but later became a central banker. They both worked extremely hard to give us a good education and told us that no one could ever take it away from us.

As a child, I once sat in my mother's classroom as she taught her students and thought what a great teacher she was and how lucky her students were to learn from her. I realized that my brother, sister, and I also had the good fortune of learning from her at home.

My father was an avid reader, and there were many books in the house. He encouraged us to read and be curious about the world around us. Watching him, reading came naturally to my siblings and me. This, in turn, helped us do well in school. My parents supported us a great deal at home; we studied hard and prepared for entrance exams for scholarships, which helped us get admitted to good schools in Sri Lanka. They found tutors for subjects that were especially challenging as we prepared for our O Level and A Level examinations. My siblings and I did very well in school and later completed our graduate work in the U.S. Today, I look back and see that the best gift my parents gave us was education. It helped us to become confident as children and later as adults, and the courage to travel to a foreign country for higher education and eventually to find fulfilling careers and lives.

My parents believed in leading a well-balanced life. So, besides working hard to achieve academic success, we learned that it was equally important to make time to go outside and play, to spend quality time with family and friends, to be kind to ourselves and others, to lend a helping hand to those who need it, to respect others, especially the many teachers who helped shape our lives, the elderly in society, and to have religious faith.

My parents lived to these values and passed them on to me; they are a fundamental part of my life and helped me achieve a full and contented life. Like my mother, I have a career in academia. Being able to teach students and impart the value of education to them is a blessing for me.

Story 21

The Value of Love and Support

By Cole Cassilas

Growing up, me and my grandfather were remarkably close. We would talk on the phone every day. My grandpa was a huge baseball fan, and at the time, I was playing baseball. He loved to come to my games and watch me play, even though he lived about two-and-a-half hours away from me.

When he wasn't able to attend my games, I would call him directly after them and tell him how it went. My grandpa was never a man with a lot of money, but he would reward me for getting hits in baseball. His reward to me was giving me a dollar per hit in my games. I really valued that growing up. Later, with failing health, when he was sick and getting worse by the day, I would go to see him, and he would always tell me that he wanted to be my agent when I made it pro.

Now, of course, I never made it that far, but I loved hearing that. I really valued all the time I had with him growing up and the long phone conversations we had.

It's something I will never forget.

Story 22

On Determination and Overcoming Fear

By Radhika Ramdev

A. Sibling Role Model: A Lesson on Determination

Follow your passion… It is easier said than done.

I often think of my brother, Rahul, who has followed his dream of becoming a pilot. He was all of 17, fresh out of high school, and knew in his heart that he wanted to fly. This was in the 1980s in Kolkata, India, when being a pilot wasn't considered a "real" career path.

After some challenges with the family and logistical and financial obstacles, he was on his path to being a pilot. He was determined and focused, almost to a point of obsession. He talked about planes, read about aircrafts, was knowledgeable about the industry, and worked for multiple airlines. I would joke with him and say if someone were to dissect his brain, it would look like a plane!

Whenever I feel I'm losing my focus in life, I try to think of how fearless and determined he has been on this journey, and it helps me find my footing. Today, as a "between 45-50"-year-old adult, I still admire his way of setting life goals and creating a better way for his family. He is a great role model, and I appreciate his dedication, honesty, and determination.

B. Overcoming Fear

I always had a fear of public speaking. Who doesn't?

Some years ago, a colleague put out a casting call for an amateur play production—for *Salome*, a tragedy by Oscar Wilde. I love theater and enjoy plays, on main stage and smaller productions. I contemplated signing up for an acting role and was nervous just thinking about it because of my fear of public speaking. But I went ahead, tried out, and was cast in a small role.

We practiced for months. Finally, the production took place in a small theater in the piano district of Boston. I was terrified, asking myself every day why I'd even put myself in this position. To overcome my fear, I reminded myself that I loved theater, and being part of this production was a very real way for me to immerse myself in it. The experience was empowering, and I felt I had conquered my fear for the moment.

Overcoming my fears is difficult, but it makes me more resilient to embrace change and experience life in a more meaningful way.

Story 23

The Value of Telling the Truth

By Adeel Koshal

Years ago, I attended a month long "Hindu Camp" in a suburb of Rochester, New York. It was similar to camps organized by various churches for children between the ages of 6 to 14 years. Besides focusing on Hinduism and its practices, a variety of sports and other recreational activities are also offered. The camp was quite popular.

After the camp was over, my mom, Bela, drove to Rochester to pick me up. According to the rules of the camp, children are not allowed to have any money or speak to their parents during their stay. However, my mom gave me some money before leaving me at the camp, thinking I might like to spend it in the soda machine or to buy stationary.

I had never tasted Coke and was curious as to its taste. So, the day Mom came to pick me up, I bought a can of Coke from the vending machine and took a sip. I did not like its taste. As we were headed home, I put the can in the car.

Mom asked me if I had spent any of the money she had given me. I said no. However, the camp administrators keep a record of the inventory and the number of sales from the vending machines. This information is shared with the parents by the camp administrators when they cleared the accounts. So, Mom knew about the transaction.

When we settled in the car and were ready to leave, Mom confronted me about spending the money on a can of Coke. I admitted I had spent the money on the Coke can and apologized for not telling the truth. Since the Coke was still in the car, Mom asked me why I hadn't finished it. I said I did not like the taste.

Mom pulled the car over on the side of the road and made me drink the entire can of Coke as a punishment for not telling the truth. I threw up after drinking it. I remember the incident well, and it just might stay in my mind forever!

So, I learned that I had to pay a price for not telling the truth. And often one lie leads to another and becomes a habit.

Story 24
The Value of Not Stealing

By Karen Vedder

I remember the one time that Vinette, my daughter, was in high school. Vinette and her friend had gone downtown, and when I picked her up, she was having cotton candy. I asked her about it; she said she had taken it from a shop she and her friend stopped at. It was clear to me that she hadn't paid for it.

I told her to get her piggy bank and take the amount of the price of candy. I drove her to the store. She gave the money to the store owner.

I wanted her to learn that she shouldn't take something without paying for it. That would be stealing.

Story 25

The Value of Creativity for a Rich Life

By Shreela Goel

Being creative and learning new things has been a part of my life. It has expanded my mind and shaped me as a non-conformist.

My mother was my role model and a unique personality. Mom did many things most women of her time did not do. She played tennis and badminton with the faculty men on campus in Sri Lanka. On Radio Ceylon, she collaborated with two Sinhalese men, who provided the music and the male voices for the Rabindranath Tagore songs Mom sang.

She taught me many things: to read and write Bengali, my mother tongue, and to sing Tagore's songs; to sew on her manual Singer sewing machine, and while she was expecting my brother, I sewed dozens of nappies (diapers), baby clothes, and bedsheets with matching pillowcases; and to embroider, encouraging me to create my own designs.

I learned to knit from Mom. My neighborhood friends and I sang as we sewed and knitted. Till today, my friends talk affectionately about my mom as they remember our childhood. A friend, now living in Australia, recalled how she would drop stitches, while learning how to knit from Mom.

In the U.S., Mom co-founded the San Francisco Bay Area's oldest and largest Bengali association today. My daughter learned Bharatanatyam, a South Indian classical dance form, and performed in dramas and songs created by Tagore. I sewed the costumes for her performances and guided other mothers to do the same, seeing it as an opportunity to socialize with the other mothers. I sewed drapes with swags and cascades to enhance the windows in our homes, saving several thousands of dollars. We were young and starting our lives in the U.S., and every cent mattered.

I studied landscaping and helped with gardens for friends. When my kids were growing up, I learned cake decoration and made special cakes for our children's birthdays and other celebrations. I painted two murals in my living room that drew the attention of visitors to my home. When my home got flooded, my daughter was reluctant to accept the $10,000 reimbursement for each mural for a painter to come and replace the artwork. She felt that if it was not my artwork, she didn't want anything done by others! Luckily, we were able to salvage the paintings.

I take pride in being "out of style" when it comes to behavior, dressing age-appropriately, and decorating my home. I do what pleases me without the need of approval from my friends or imitating the current decors in houses.

Creativity is an essential and large part of my life. Through it, I have made friends whose company I have enjoyed throughout my life.

Story 26

The Value in Serving

By Jatindra Kumar Dewan

In 1956, I joined the Indian School of Mines, Dhanbad, in the state of Bihar (now Jharkand) in India, for a four-year course in mining engineering. Admission to the institute was based on the results of a competitive written examination, conducted all over India. Some states offered scholarships to prospective candidates based on the results of this examination. The name of the Indian School of Mines (ISM) has now been changed to Indian Institute of Technology (IIT). Based in and having studied in Calcutta, I appeared for the examinations in Calcutta. I came first and was offered a scholarship for the next four years. This covered the fees and also included a stipend, which took care of the board and lodging in the hostel and of other related expenses.

When I started my studies, I was given a room and a choice of a Mess (a term used then for various cafeterias spread out on the campus) for my meals. On the first day, I met Krishan Kumar, a fellow student from Delhi, who was in the room next to me; we had opted for the same Mess. Kumar and I became friends and would go to the Mess together for meals. We went for evening walks.

I learned that Kumar came from a family with humble beginnings and that his father had a roadside bookshop in Delhi. Three months into the course, Kumar realized that he could not afford to bear the expenses of the school. He wanted to leave the institution, although he was a good student, especially in drawing and practical work.

Some of us tried to persuade him to stay back and complete his course work. But Kumar was helpless, and he requested the authorities if he could quit and leave the mining college. I was very moved by his situation and offered to support him for his essential expenses from my scholarship money. Kumar agreed, reluctantly.

I started paying for Kumar's tuition and Mess expenses. My parents, who could very well afford to take care of all my expenses, objected to my decisions and action. However, I convinced them that if I had not earned my scholarship, would they not have paid for my education at the institute?

55

In 1960, Kumar and I both got our degrees in Mining Engineering. Kumar then joined Indian Railways and retired as Chief Mining Engineer. His and his family did well and had a happy life.

The moral of my story is that help to the right person and at the right time could be beneficial to them and their families, of course, with God's Grace.

Story 27

Value of Helping the Poor and Enabling Livelihoods

By Jatindra Kumar Dewan

After I retired as Managing Director of Williamson Magor Company in Kolkata, India, my wife and I moved to Gurgaon—a suburb of New Delhi—where we bought a house. After many years in a very full-time job, there was a vacuum in my life. I had time on my hands. My wife Nalini and I wanted to do something constructive.

We began to offer free tutorial classes in English and computers for the underprivileged school children between the ages of 14-20 years residing in the neighboring villages. We wanted to help them in becoming proficient in the above-mentioned subjects, so that they could improve their grades and choose promising careers that could ensure financial stability in the long run.

One of the young men, Lala Ram, was in Class 10 in the Chakarpur Village School. He joined both of our tutorial classes. He was punctual and keen to learn, goal oriented to do well and to make a bright future for himself and his family. His father worked as a laborer/worker in the nearby fields.

One day, Lala Ram stopped coming to our tutorial classes. We learned from his classmates that he was seriously sick and hospitalized. He was diabetic, and doctors advised him to temporarily quit school and rest at home. He was also advised two to three doses of insulin shots twice daily, something his family could not afford.

My wife and I visited him at his home and took him to the private clinic. The diagnosis was the same: insulin to manage his diabetes. Since it was a long-term treatment, we realized that we couldn't pay for the entire treatment. Another challenge was how to store the insulin in their home, as the family had no refrigerator.

We bought a small battery-operated refrigerator for his home and made sure it was working properly. We also bought several vaccines of insulin and stored in that refrigerator. A medical practitioner friend agreed to visit Lala Ram's house twice daily and give the shots. Lala Ram recovered, resumed his studies, and graduated from high school. Later, we helped him to get admission at the university, where he excelled, too.

We wanted to help further Lala Ram in getting a job, and therefore requested a friend who had a manufacturing unit in New Delhi if he could help and employ him. Our friend offered Lala Ram a job. He quickly picked up the tricks of the trade and excelled at the job. He later earned well, which helped him to take care of his entire family.

Lala is happily married today with a wife who also has a bachelor's degree. His hard work and dedication paid off, and so did our efforts.

For my wife and me, it was a great feeling of satisfaction and a unique experience that we could help someone in need. We saw it as "seva," or service. We feel fortunate and especially blessed by the Almighty God that we got this opportunity, motivation, and strength for doing this task.

Story 28

The Value of Faith, Devotion, Duty, and Sacrifice

By Sandee Bishman

I was 11 years old when I started helping my father to care for my mother, who was recovering from a surgery to remove kidney stones. When I was 13, my mother developed uterine cancer and had surgery to remove the tumors. Once again, I cared for her and took on many household duties, as my sister was five years old.

A few years later, my mother had another kidney surgery, during which she contracted a staph infection. I spent a whole year caring for her while raising a four-year-old daughter, who could have easily picked up the infection. My mother died in 2010.

My husband had three surgeries for stomach ulcers. Caring for him and raising a child was a definite strain. I lost my husband to dementia and Parkinson's in 2012. Before this medical challenge, my daughter was diagnosed with invasive ductal carcinoma at the age of 39, in 2007. She had two daughters, and I often traveled to Columbus, Ohio (61 miles), several times a week to give her a hand. Thankfully, she was in fairly good health, even with receiving chemo every month.

In 2015, my sister, who was single, asked me to come to Cincinnati, Ohio (124 miles from my home), to help her. Her health progressively got worse, and she was diagnosed with lung cancer. Putting my life on hold, I left my home for seven-and-a-half months to care for her until her death in 2016.

Five months after my sister died, my father died from cancer. In January 2018, my daughter died, as a result of her metastatic breast cancer, which affected her liver. She was on and tolerated chemotherapy for 10 years. What a warrior.

In January 2019, my companion of 20 years was diagnosed with aggressive small cell lung cancer which had gone to his brain. Of the four tumors, one was removed surgically, followed by radiation treatments, followed by rounds of two chemo drugs and immunotherapy treatments. After seven months, his cancer is gone, but he will need immunotherapy treatments for the rest of his life or till the drug does not keep the cancer arrested. Thanks to God our Father, he has no cancer.

How did I survive during all these adversities? Through a tremendous faith in my Lord Jesus Christ, who gave me will power. Plus, prayers and love from many supporters and my love for all these family members helped me to continue. I feel God put me on this Earth to love and care for others, which I will do until He calls me home to His kingdom!

Story 29

The Value in Learning and Perseverance

By Manjulika Koshal

My husband and I have a home in Bangalore, India, which we visit from December to March every year. Twenty-eight-year-old Parvati is our household staff person. This is a story of Parvati.

Since we bought the home 10 years ago, Parvati has been with us. Even though we are in Bangalore only for three months of the year, we pay her for all 12 months. She has learned how to keep the house as we like it; is honest; and has a set of keys to the house. When we are at Bangalore, Parvati comes to our home thrice a day: from 7:00 to 8:00 AM; 12:00 to 2:00 PM; and again 4:00 to 6:30 PM. She has a full day from 7:00 AM to 7:00 PM, working in two other homes besides ours.

Parvati is single, lives with her mother, and is surrounded by family scattered all over the city of Bangalore. She does not have any formal education but can read, write, and sign her name in Kannada, the local language. She was keen to learn English, and I taught her the alphabets, and now, she can read words. Parvati's willingness to learn extends to other areas too, be it a language, a good habit, cooking, home decoration, and household management skills, such as organizing closets.

Parvati was extremely interested to tell her story and consulted her mother, too. This story was narrated by her in Hindi, an official language of India.

Growing up in my home, there was a tradition to drink a glass of lukewarm water with a few drops of lemon, the first thing in the morning, on empty stomach. I have continued this to the present time and even convinced my husband to join me. Every morning, we both drink lemon water followed by an additional glass of regular water. This helps to clear our bowels, and recently, many studies have shown that besides many other health benefits of lemon, it helps in building immunity, too. I introduced this ritual to Parvati.

Every morning at 7:00 AM at Bangalore, I prepared three glasses of lemon water and Parvati, my husband, and I have been drinking it on an empty stomach. I encouraged Parvati to start this ritual for her 65-year-old mother, who is severely constipated and takes allopathic medicines whose side effects are nausea and vomiting.

After a week of the lemon water ritual, Parvati realized its benefits and started preparing lemon water at home for her mother and herself. It worked for her mother, too, so much so, that when she went to visit her son and his family, she took one lemon from home. Upon arrival, she told her son and daughter-in-law to drink lemon water first thing in the morning, as it was effective for constipation.

Parvati noted her mother's action and was impressed by her faith and belief in the benefits of the lemon water ritual. Parvati was happy and thankful to us for introducing her to the ritual to her and eventually, to her mother.

In another incident, Parvati, when she started working with us 10 years ago, took four teaspoonfuls of sugar in one cup of tea. We asked her if her mother was diabetic, and she said, "Not only diabetic but has high blood pressure, too." So, we suggested she try tea without sugar. In the beginning, she resisted a bit. But soon, she asked me to reduce the amount of sugar in her tea slowly without telling her. I did this till one day she had a cup of tea without any sugar. She was happy and is now sugar free.

I wanted to share these two incidents, as for me it shows that if you honestly believe in something, God gives you the strength and willpower to carry out that mission and ultimately you succeed.

Story 30

The Satisfaction in Helping the Helpless

By Jatindra Kumar Dewan

After retiring from the Williamson Magor Company in Calcutta, India, Nalini, my wife, and I bought a home in Gurgaon, a suburb of New Delhi, where mostly retired executives lived. A beautiful neighborhood with modern facilities, the community has home delivery and home visitation services for various facilities, including a physiotherapy center, managed by a young woman, Naina. These services are a boon for senior citizens.

Naina from the physiotherapy center is from Varanasi, a town in North India, and the daughter of a village mailman. Once, Naina's father, a chronic heart patient, was visiting her and got terribly ill. Naina was visibly shaken by his illness, sharing with Nalini and me her father's condition.

We scheduled an appointment for Naina's father with a renowned cardiologist, Dr. Padmavati, at Kailash Colony in New Delhi, who recommended immediate heart surgery. Her father was admitted to hospital, and the total cost of the surgery and post-surgery recovery in hospital was about Rupees 3 lakhs. Naina could not afford this.

The hospital expected the full amount up front. Even though my wife and I wanted to help Naina and her father, we realized that we could only help with 50 percent of the amount. We raised the rest of the money from friends.

Next, the hospital required blood donations. Once again, we approached our friends, and several donated blood for the surgery. With the help of our niece and the son of a close friend, the required amount of blood was collected.

Finally, Naina's father had the surgery, which was successful. After 10 days, he needed a hygienic place to stay for at least a month. Naina's house was not suitable for post-surgery care. A close friend came to the rescue. She offered for a month, one part of the wing of her large house for Naina and her father, including meals and any other help.

This worked well. Naina's father recovered successfully and moved back to his hometown after getting clearance from the hospital.

This has been one of the most rewarding experience of our lives. My wife and I were deeply moved by this incident and till this day, it is a constant reminder to us about what "giving" truly means. Giving is not so much of donating money to temples and churches; rather, it constitutes "a genuine service imparted to a needy human being." The rewards from this kind of giving brings a special joy to both parties that no treasure of the world can beat. This is giving in the true sense of the term.

Story 31

The Life of my Mother

By Nalini Dewan

My mother Satya Badhwar was born and educated in the best schools and colleges in Delhi. Her father was a power engineer, well known for setting up new power plants for electrification purposes. He did well and owned his own house. Her mother was religious and known for helping the poor and needy. She had three brothers and three sisters.

My mother was beautiful and at the age of 21 was married to my father, who was from a business family that owned five or six cotton and ginning mills, spread over different parts of India. My grandfather was the chief head of the entire business. He was like the CEO, and everyone took orders from him. He was also a well-educated engineer.

My father was the oldest of his siblings of four brothers and four sisters. All were educated in different parts of India and England. My father was head of a cotton mill at Moga in Punjab. My mother Satya took over the responsibility of bringing up my father's siblings in addition to the household duties.

Over time, my mother gave birth to twins—myself and my brother Prabodh. Later, our younger brother Lalit was born. We were a happy family of five.

As we grew up, I got married to a well-educated mining engineer working in western India with a British firm. My twin brother got married to a girl from Punjab, and the younger brother, who had joined the Indian Army, got married to a girl from U.P.

Both my brothers and their families moved to Delhi, and both moved into my parents' home. Soon after this incident, my father fell ill, and he passed away within a week of hospitalization.

My mother was 75 years old and not really able to manage the house with two families living with her in her home. Both daughters-in-law did not like to look after my mother and began neglecting her. She was compelled to stay in her room, not even allowed to go into her kitchen for a glass of water or a cold drink from the refrigerator; not to mention meals or a cup of tea. She was locked into her room from the outside, and her medical needs such as high blood pressure, diabetes, and heart related problems were ignored.

One day, I decided to bring her to my home for good in Gurgaon about 20 kilometers away. Luckily and reluctantly, my mother agreed. She brought with her only one small bag and left behind all other items in the very house that she and her husband owned.

At our home, my mother had an independent, well-furnished, air-conditioned room with an attached bath. She enjoyed eating meals with other members of the family on the dining table. Not restricted to one room living, she moved around the house freely. She also enjoyed going for morning and evening walks in the garden with a helper who was specially hired for her. As she was fond of flowers, she looked forward to these walks and enjoyed strolling in the midst of flower-laden bushes in the garden. Special care was taken to provide her medical aid and medicines as per need.

It's unfortunate and sad that her two sons and their families couldn't give her the respect, comfort, and love she needed in her old age. She had sacrificed a great deal, taking care of my father's side of the family, as well as raising us children. She deserved better.

The change of scene helped my mother. She was happy and treated with respect. She started going out and attended religious groups of musical gatherings.

She lived happily and passed away peacefully at the age of 92. She was given an appropriate send off by family and friends. I feel blessed that I was able to bring my mom out of the trenches and see her face once again smiling and contented. I am also thankful to the Almighty God to have given me an opportunity for spending some quality time with my mother during her last golden years of life.

What I have learned from this experience is that the influence, the teachings and the inspirations received from one's parents are a valuable treasure that shapes your life, and at any cost, one should never ever neglect one's parents.

Story 32

The Nature of Values

By Bhanu Kapil

I am writing this as its almost dusk. It's late spring, and I am in England, where I was born and where I am living again after having been in the United States for many years.

A year ago, I would have said that I valued creativity. As a writer, it would be strange, for example, not to place value on writing. We were living in Colorado where I had raised my son. My mother fell ill, and we decided to relocate to England, where she and I are citizens.

So, I find myself in a small city in eastern England, surprised I'm homesick for the American west and the daily, ordinary, consistent contact with the people around me, in my neighborhood, at home, or in my workplace.

I valued the creativity of my students too. Is a classroom a kind of laboratory for experimental practice or thought, or is it the real experiment, a substantial openness and trust in the company of other human beings? I treasure the insights, the connections, and the wildness of my time as a teacher, something that brings value to my decision to leave my birthplace and explore life in a country that is not, and perhaps never will be, my own.

A year ago, I would have said that what I valued was caring for my mother at home. But the truth is that I was exhausted, and it was overwhelming to live in a country in which health care (for a non-citizen) came at a considerable cost.

It is a relief to be in a country with nationalized health care, and so I think, as it turns out, that I value that. I value the NHS (National Health System) and the culture of care that we have been a part of since returning. And yes, though it is harder for me to distinguish duty and value, caring for my mother (with my sister, at home) has changed my character.

I value my mother's stories, her rhythms, and everything I have yet to learn from her: how to make an onion masala for toor daal, how to crochet a crescent moon, how we came to be the people we are, how creativity and survival are perhaps the same things. Yes, I value the elders in the Punjabi community, the generation that lived through Partition. It is why I agreed to travel to Ohio last year, to be with you all, and am so glad I did. In your company, my heart opened wide.

I want to place value for the rest of my life, whatever there is left of it, on love. What it is to be with others and to listen to them, whether or not that results in a product or a cultural artifact of some kind. Perhaps I will never write another poem! That is alright.

Story 33

Helping Others and Staying Calm

By Rajindar Koshal

A. HELPING OTHERS WHENEVER YOU CAN

I was in the sixth or seventh grade and doing well at school. After doing my homework, I used to play until dinnertime. One day, my mother said that after my homework, I should help our domestic staff's son, who was in the third grade and not doing well in school. I was a little reluctant. My mother said: "My son, education is such a gift that the more you share it, the more it increases; nobody can steal it from you. So, by teaching and sharing it, you will also gain more education."

I was impressed by what my mother said. The next day, I started tutoring the boy. At the end of the academic year, he was well prepared and confident and passed his final exam with good grades.

B. RESPOND TO ANGER WITH CALM

In 1986, my wife and I hired a reputed contractor to do the expansion and renovation of our home. The agreement was that the payment would be made in parts, as and when the work progressed. During this time, once we were going out of town and leaving for the airport. The contractor came over and asked me to go over the invoice and write a check. I told him that this would be possible only after we return. He got quite angry and started shouting at the top of his voice. I kept my cool and told him that I would pay him after I return. We left without further discussion.

After I returned, I went to the contractor's office and asked him to show me the invoice. I found it was inflated and asked him to recheck it. Rechecking the invoice, he found he had overcharged and corrected the invoice. I wrote a check for the correct amount and gave to him, or Bob, as we called him.

I said to Bob, "Being angry and rude comes at a cost, but being cool and kind benefits us in the long run."

He got up and hugged me and said, "Dr. Koshal, from today onwards I am going to follow your advice in dealing with people."

Since then, whenever I have met Bob, he is cool and respectful.

Story 34

On Hypocrisy and Wishes Coming True

By Rajindar Koshal

A. THE HYPOCRISY AT A PLACE OF WORSHIP

When I was 32 years old, I fasted every Tuesday, and returning home from office stopped by a temple to offer sweets. I enjoyed this ritual and offered whatever I could afford.

One day, there was quite a rush at the temple, and the waiting line for offerings was long. I stood in line for a while. Suddenly, the priest came over to me took me to the front of the line. I was curious as to why he was doing this. I looked around and noticed that all the others in line had offerings of less value than mine.

I realized that the priest gave preference to those who were offering more than others. I felt this was wrong, as in the place of worship, we are all equal. I returned home and told my father what had happened and that I would continue with my fast but not go to the temple. My father approved of my decision.

Now, I refuse to visit a temple where the entrance might be based on one's status or wealth.

B. WHEN A WISH COMES TRUE

You might laugh after you have read this story of my odd wish.

As a teenager in India, I was an observer of the "arranged marriage" system—a marriage arranged for the young man and woman by the parents, extended families, and matchmakers. Here, the young man and his family had the upper hand. They would visit the home of the woman to check out their status and the details of the woman—her qualifications, cooking skills, and her appearance and personality. The young man had the prerogative to say yes or no to the proposed life partner. I saw this situation often and the pain it caused the woman when she was rejected. I have seen this in the U.S., too.

However, in the last 15 years, things are changing. As more women are going for higher education and becoming economically independent, they are either opting for delaying their marriages and finding on their own a suitable life partner later, or they are having an equal role in the decision-making process of an arranged marriage system (if the parents want to go through this route). In the latter case, women are introduced to various prospective men for her future life partner. This development is more prevalent among the middle-class Indian families where both parents and daughters have a broader outlook on life.

As a teenager, I wished that I would marry only when I had a car and that I would meet only one woman and select her as my life partner. With the grace of the Almighty, today, I can say that when I was 34 years old, my both wishes were fulfilled.

I was able to have my life partner by meeting only one woman. However, in my case, my wife was well educated, had a Ph.D., and was teaching at a university. And her parents were liberal. My future wife and I met in a separate room and frankly shared our expectations and how our goals might be affected if we married. Back then, it was unheard of to permit such a meeting between the prospective couple. We are married now for the last 55 years.

Story 35

The Value of a Substantial Life

By Anita Anand

I grew up in a privileged home in rural West Bengal in India during the 1950s and 60s. My father was a mining engineer in charge of the deepest coal mines in Asia, called Chinakuri Pits 1 and 2.

He began his career in Andrew Yule and Company, a British company with diverse businesses. As my father rose in the ranks of the company, most senior managers were British. We socialized with them and their families and became rather anglicized. My two older sisters and I went to a school run by Irish Catholic nuns of the Order of Loreto, where the medium of instruction was English. We celebrated our birthdays with cakes, balloons, paper hats and whistles. There were barbeques and cookouts with grilled meats and jacket potatoes.

Growing up, I noted my father's generosity, especially towards to those who had less than us; of which, there were plenty. In the immediate family, my father supported the education of some of his brothers and their children, assisting them in locating jobs and careers. Others came asking for assistance with employment, and my father helped whenever he could. He watched out for the underdog, starting with those around us. The company generously gave us staff, and my father supported the education of their children and made sure they were well settled in life.

My father lived life large. Generously and lovingly, he indulged us in our whims and fancies as children and later when we were older. Rather than tell us how we should live our lives, his life was a model for us. He worked and played hard. There was much socializing with food and drink; there were picnics and holidays with family and friends. We travelled, learned to play tennis, to swim, and to ride horses. My father was a member of a yacht club, and we went sailing on the River Maithon, on many weekends. He enjoyed a drink and loved to smoke.

Like most middle-class men of his time, my father saw great value in education and encouraged my sisters and me to get formal education, have a career, and be financially independent. From him, I learned that the joy of life was in giving—in work and society. His generosity always amazed me.

As an adult, I have and continue to live life large, like him. I like the good life, challenging work, good friends, and helping others with my time and energy. I have high levels of trust, faith in people, and an optimistic look on life. These all, I believe, I have inherited from my father.

Story 36

The Importance of
Education, Perseverance, and Adaptability

By Shreela Goel

My father came from large family of humble beginnings. He was one of the first group of students to get a Ph.D. from Patna University, winning a gold medal for his studies. He got a DLitt (Doctor of Literature) under the British system of education, conferred on him by the eminent philosopher and the President of India, Dr. Sarvapalli Radhakrishnan.

My father's work brought him close to an academician at the University of New Mexico, the Indian Philosophical Conferences, and this association and friendship brought our family to the United States in 1964, when my father was offered a Visiting Professorship at the University of New Mexico. That was the start of our lives in the U.S.A., where we have lived since then.

My mother was well educated for her time, with a Masters' degree in English Literature and a minor in Mathematics before she married my father. Her future mother-in-law commented, "What good is it to have an educated girl come into the family if she cannot cook?" Regardless of this, my dad met her for the second time a year later, said it was meant to be. He overlooked his mother's objections and married my mom. Mom got along with her in-laws and was admired and looked up to by the entire family.

Every seven years, the University of Ceylon, where Dad taught, sent faculty, along with their family, to England for post-doctoral research. I was four years old on our first trip. Mom started a degree in Psychology at Bedford College at the University of London. She finished that degree when we returned seven years later.

I was 11 years old the second time around, and my brother was two. He refused to learn English or go to nursery school but enjoyed watching children's shows on TV. Mom being a psychologist understood this reluctance and didn't force him to go to nursery school. She and Dad decided that they would take turns going to the university and care for him at home.

Dad took care of my brother during the day, taking him for walks for shopping for daily supplies on Portobello Road. My brother would unconsciously reply in English to the people he met! Dad did the housework, including cooking, and serving us morning coffee in bed during the cold winter mornings in London. This way, Mom had all the time she needed to study. Dad attended seminars, interfaced with his colleagues, and did his research when Mom was back from college.

From my parents, I learned that perseverance and determination are important to achieve one's life goals, especially during difficult situations in life. They showed me how to adapt by setting a good example. They inspired me to study further after I got married and had children.

Story 37

The Value of Accepting All Religions

By Shreela Goel

Growing up in Sri Lanka on the Peradeniya campus of the University of Ceylon, we had a Sinhalese Buddhist family on one side of our home and a Hindu Tamil family on the other. With the Sinhalese family, I went to the temple, dressed in my white school uniform on their special days, and prayed with them. I also prayed with the Hindu family, even though I did not understand the language. At my convent school, I went to church with my Catholic friends.

Every seven years, professors in the University of Ceylon travelled to London on a sabbatical leave for post-doctoral research. My family went, too, and I was fortunate to attend nursery and grammar school in London. The school day started with the principal reading a chapter from the Bible, after which we sang hymns. In class, we read the Old Testament, but when I saw that Jewish girls were excused, I managed to get out of class, too. I practiced the piano during that period.

Now, every Christmas, we go to a nearby church. My kids were small when we went for the first time. I knew and sang all the hymns. My kids had never heard me sing these before. They sang the Christmas carols they had heard during the holiday season.

Years later, after the untimely death of my mother due to a car accident, I was doing my Ph.D. under my father, as he wanted me to continue maintaining the new editions of his publications. From his philosopher's perspective, I got an overview of Hinduism and other world religions. My parents followed a non-ritualistic but philosophical practice of Hinduism, which is actually "a way of life" rather than a religion per se. I found my father's teachings too abstract for my "scientifically-oriented" brain to comprehend. I had been trained to observe before I concluded anything.

My father told me that I would understand these concepts as I matured— that in transcendental philosophy there is something beyond this world and universe; that the power or force running this universe should remain nameless, and the moment we name it, we are missing and limiting it.

Once, lecturing at the University of New Mexico, my father said there is no God. He described the "power" in negative terms as being indescribable or did not say what exactly is running this universe. He said there was an "eye behind the eye that makes us see," and an "ear behind the ear that makes us hear." He explained that the mere structures of the organs do not make us see or hear, but there is something in the background that lets us see and hear. The mere mixture of chemicals did not result in life. There is a powerful force that has allowed the universe, as we know it, to exist and all the life forms to get generated.

Over time, as I matured, I have come to know that there is, indeed, a certain power that is within each being and beyond our universe the way we know it, and that we don't have to go to any particular place to worship because it is within us.

I realized that I could pray, or not, and could contemplate or meditate at home, in a temple, a mosque, synagogue, or on the mountains. My father said: Learn about all the religions of the world, accept, and revere them, but leave them and do what makes you comfortable. Lead your life in a way without hurting anyone.

I live my life this way without any guilt or fear. In my travels to different countries with various religious practices, I follow the rules of the places of worship, believing that no matter what the religion, it is a place for paying homage to that Divine superior power that controls everything around us.

This, I learned from my parents.

Story 38

The Value of
Perseverance, Hard Work, and Dedication

By Chandra Akkhial

The year was 1969, in a beautiful town in the southeastern state of Tennessee in the United States. I sat in my graduation gown, watching the line of graduates go to the podium, one by one, to receive their honored degrees. Waiting for my turn, I had a feeling of accomplishment. The hustle and bustle of the crowd and the laughter of my fellow graduates accelerated my feelings of an achiever. I was on cloud nine.

Next day, after the ceremony, I looked at my degree and thought: *How did I do this?* This question took me back to the first few days of my coming to the U.S.A., with just a few dollars in my pocket. Wandering around on the lawns of the university campus, not knowing a soul, I had mixed emotions. *Will I be able to survive here? Will I be able to adjust in this strange land? Will I be homesick? How am I going to manage with a handful of dollars?*

With these questions, I decided to meet the Dean of the college. Next day, when I went to his office, he asked: "Chandra, what can I do for you?"

I said, "I need money."

He reached into his pocket and took out a handful of hundred-dollar bills, saying, "Will this be enough for you for the time being?"

I smiled, nodded, and thanked him.

I felt happy, safe, and secure. I knew my assistantship money would be available to me soon.

I was fortunate to get scholarships all through my academic career. I came to Nashville, Tennessee on an assistantship. Besides the academic challenge, I was in an apartment with four other students. There was one single room, and two doubles. By lottery, I got the single room. Then there was the food. In those days, Americans were mostly non-vegetarian. I was a vegetarian, but I learned to make meals with varieties of cheese, tomatoes, onions, green chilies, and tomato ketchup. I lived on these for two years till I graduated.

My home, father, and siblings back in India were on my mind. My father had a limited income, and we were a large family of 10 (four brothers and four sisters, plus the parents), but we managed to enjoy life. Growing up, I never thought it was a struggle.

My father had one bicycle that we all had to share it. My turn came only when the bicycle had a flat tire, as I was good in repairing it. Oh, what a joy it was when the bicycle needed repairs, and it was handed over to me. I was so happy to use the bicycle for a few hours when it was with me after I had repaired it.

I compared my life in the U.S.A. to that of mine in my hometown and began to use my scholarship money frugally. Every month, I sent money to my father. I also got a job at Marshall University right after graduation.

In 1970, I got married. It was a happy life, and we had two bright children. My expenses increased when we bought a home and needed a budget for a family of four. But I managed to live within my means, saving and sending money diligently to my father every month as my sisters had to be married, and my father needed help.

Today, I am an Emeritus Professor of Economics from Marshall University. Retired with an active academic life, I started a four-year degree college in my hometown in Dharwad in the state of Karnataka in India. My two sons got a good education in reputed schools—John Hopkins and MIT—and are owners of a successful IT company with 40 workers in Bangalore, India, and a branch at Seattle, Washington state, U.S.A.

The story of my life is one of perseverance, hard work, dedication, and sacrifice. I learned the value of these.

Story 39

The Determination to End a Regressive Tradition

By Priti Rao

My grandmother, whom we called Nani, was a blue-eyed beauty, who stood five feet tall and was born more than a century back to a family who doted on daughters. Her father was a judge at the Agra High Court in India. She was married at the age of 13 into a family of doctors, and even though she was illiterate, she was intelligent and picked up fast from others around her, adapting to her surroundings.

She travelled to visit her daughter (my mother). Often, she would travel by plane by herself without being able to read or understand the English announcements. I was about 10 years old and wondered about how she managed. But my bold and determined Nani was confident that she would be able to manage.

After her first flight, I asked her how she had managed to get through security and on to the correct flight.

"All I did," she explained with her beautiful smile, "was to identify a foreigner, and ask, 'Agra?'" she said. "If she nodded yes, I would sit next to her, and as soon as she got up, I got up, too, and followed her to the plane."

I asked her why she had asked a foreigner.

"Arey," she said, "beta sare angrez Taj dekhane toh jate hain!" (Oh, my child, all foreigners go to see the Taj).

The eldest daughter-in-law of the family, Nani was born on Dhanteras (two days before Diwali), so was named Dhanwanti, or the goddess of wealth. She married Pitaji (my grandfather), a man with strong Gandhian principles. Pitaji was 18 years old when he married Nani. He studied to be a teacher, and then went on to become the head of the department of Chemistry at Agra College.

My grandparents lived in a joint family, and the women kept a 'ghunghat' or a veil that covered their face from the elderly men in the family. My Nani said it was the legacy left by the Muslim rulers, as their women wore the burkha, so the Hindu women started to cover their faces, too, with the corners of their sarees called a "paloo." This, over time, became a tradition, which continues in parts of Rajasthan, Haryana, Uttar Pradesh, and other northern Indian states. Pitaji was against this tradition and often urged Nani to get rid of it.

Nani, after toying with the idea, decided to visit her father and consult him about this issue. She returned a week later with determination to "break traditions," she said.

The next day, she walked out of her room without a ghunghat, a bold step, which left the elders' plan.

"I had to implement it," she told me, her voice shaking as if she were in that moment, "I didn't know if it would work or not, but I had a silent supporter in your grandfather, and that was enough for me." When I asked her whether she was scared, she said, "Of course, I was scared, I could not sleep the whole night, thinking of what course of events would follow the next day. It's next to impossible to tell why people were totally stunned. I didn't know whether they were staring at my beauty (which they had not seen so far), or were staring at me because I had broken the tradition!" she triumphantly told me.

"What about Pitaji?" I asked her.

"What about him? I saw him from the corner of my eye, secretly smiling and trying to assess the situation," she said, her eyes wandering, trying to picture Pitaji's face from decades back.

Even though she was frightened, she just stood with her head bowed down. She was waiting for them to ask her why she had decided to take this step, as her answer was well rehearsed and practiced. Pitaji was waiting for a witty yet effective reply from her. She had to make it sound as if the step was taken in order to benefit the whole family.

So, she said, "Everyone in Agra who knows me is making fun of me and our family. Agra is also my 'myke,' or my father's house, and everyone has seen my face before marriage. I will not tolerate that my 'sasural,' or husband's household, is made fun of just because I am made to wear a ghunghat, so I have decided that I will not wear it anymore. I want the whole city to respect our family."

That was the end of a regressive tradition in our family. Whenever I see women still in purdah, I secretly thank Pitaji's faith in my Nani's wit and determination.

Story 40

Value of Learning About the Fragility of Life

By Rajindar K. Koshal

In 1941, my father was the principal or headmaster (as they were called in those days) of a reputed high school in a medium-sized town called Kasur, in the south of Lahore, now in Pakistan.

My parents, two siblings, and I lived in a large house with a huge courtyard in the center surrounded by rooms. Life was carefree, smooth, and pleasant. I was nine years old and had many friends. The neighbors, mostly Muslims, were friendly and cordial.

It was August 1947, and the schools were closed for the summer holidays. I had passed class eight with good grades. As a part of the British legacy of leaving India, the Indian subcontinent was "partitioned," or divided into three areas: India, East Pakistan, and West Pakistan. Pakistan was created on August 14, and India got independence on August 15. The partition suggested that India was for the Hindus and Pakistan for Muslims.

We learned that Kasur would be in Pakistan. What followed was a tale of horror for me; my family and 2 million Hindus and Muslims who were killed and 14 million who were displaced.

There was fear of violence. My father's Muslim friends assured us that they would protect us. Next evening, the same friends requested us to leave, as they felt they would not be able to protect us should there be mobs of rioters roaming the city. In the morning, we noticed that many families were on our terrace, trying to enter our house. Our neighbor asked us to move into his home. We did.

Next day, the situation was worse. It was decided to send the women and children to Ferozepur in India, about 35 miles from Kasur. I stayed back with my father. We men spent the night awake, keeping watch with only one gun, should rioting crowds approach our area.

The situation was becoming serious, and we needed to leave Kasur as soon as possible. Luckily, we were able to leave the next day in a caravan of Military trucks arranged by the Indian government. On the way, we were stopped by the Pakistan Military, but after about 30 minutes of negotiations, we were on our way. We crossed the border of Pakistan and arrived at Ferozepur, India, where curfew was imposed. Some of us were taken to a vacant school compound. Later in the evening, we were given raw lentils and rice. Fortunately, one of the staff of my father and his wife were also in the crowd, and she collected some wood from the surrounding area and cooked the food for us, too.

I realized we were now "refugees" from Pakistan. Next day, when the curfew lifted, my father and I went in search of our other family members. We found them, and all of us walked to the Ferozepur railway station. We boarded the train, thinking it would take us to New Delhi.

Around 7:00 PM, as the train approached Ludhiana station, we saw that the whole town was on fire. At the station, it was announced that as there was rioting and killing in New Delhi station, the train will not go further. We all slept that night on the platform of Ludhiana station. Next morning, the train for Delhi resumed, and we started our journey again.

Some Sikhs and Hindus approached my father and asked him to prove he was a Hindu. My father recited the "Gayatri Mantra," which is one of the earliest "Vedic text written between 1800 and 1500 BCE." It is an important Divine mantra praising the Almighty and praying for the wellbeing of all. Almost all Hindus recite this often and are well-versed with this Mantra.

As the condition in Delhi was still serious, we decided to avoid Delhi and go to Patiala instead, where the situation was calm. One has to transfer to another train from Rajpura junction to go to Patiala. We, therefore, boarded another train from Rajpura for Patiala. In Patiala, we went to my father's friend, Vayidji Ji, where we were welcomed. We felt safe and comfortable. However, after a week of our stay, it was announced that all transportations in northern India were indefinitely discontinued.

During our four months of stay in Patiala, we used to hear the news of Hindus and Sikhs being massacred in Pakistan, and the same was being done to Muslims in India. At the smallest rumor or provocation, people were killing each other.

After some time, we learned that the Muslims in Patiala had acquired a large amount of ammunition. Many rich Muslims families lived in several large houses with entrance doors like fortresses. Hindus had nothing, and each Sikh had just a sword required by their religion. So, from the fortress houses, for several days, firing continued day and night, and both Hindus and Sikhs were killed. I also heard that finally the Military of the State of Patiala came with tanks and broke the gates of the fortified houses. Then, mobs from both sides began killing each other. This went on for several days. Finally, the massacre stopped.

I went with my father to only one house, where several bodies were lying. The blood was flowing in the drain. I recall a horrible and frightening sight where a person was still breathing and begging to be killed.

I also heard that in Pakistan, Hindu, and Sikh women were stripped of their clothes and made to parade in public. The same was done to Muslim women in Patiala. There was a great loss of human lives and of human dignity everywhere.

We had been staying in Patiala for the last four months, and it was already the first week of December. The condition remained the same, and still there was no transportation in service.

Our other relatives in Delhi were getting worried for us. They did not know if we were alive or not. Radio announcements helped to locate and re-unite people who had come from Pakistan. One day, some friends of Vayidji heard our name on the radio and told us that our relatives were looking for us. Finally, our maternal uncle, who used to be one of the Cabinet members in the state of Patiala, arranged for Military trucks to give us a ride to Delhi. On December 22, we left for New Delhi and joined our relatives to start a new life.

I learned several lessons during this exceedingly difficult time. From my father, his ability to be calm. I learned that life can be fragile, and in the blink of an eye, life can go from comfort to poverty, from high status to nothing, from being in a lavish home to being on the streets. In seconds, friends can become foes. A mob mentality is gruesome. It is blind. Men turn into beasts.

And finally, even if we study, work hard, and build a life of plenty and comfort, in no time, it can fall apart, like a house of cards.

Story 41

The Value of Meditation

By Aparna Akkhial

I am the youngest of five children in my family and the only daughter. I had a very sheltered upbringing. My parents tell me that as a baby I cried a lot, woke up with bad dreams and did not sleep well. I was also hyperactive.

This could have been the reason my father initiated me into the practice of meditation at an early age. At first, I resented it, but out of respect for him, I did what I was told. My mother, too, encouraged me to meditate. My parents led a very disciplined life. My father was a man of few words, mostly silent, engaged in meditation and reading scriptures in his retirement years. I do not remember disobeying him any time.

After my marriage, I came to the U.S.A. and continued my education. It was difficult adjusting to a new environment, to a heavy workload and socializing. I was raising two children in a western environment while trying to impart Indian values. It was a lot of pressure, and I let go of my meditation routine.

When our first son Anup went to college at the age of 16, I worried about his future and his newfound freedom in an atmosphere of a different value system. I was afraid, anxious, apprehensive, and soon depressed. I resumed my meditation and slowly was able to control my mind and emotions and concentrate on what I was doing. I started feeling mentally strong. My self-confidence increased.

I now lead a more meaningful, peaceful, and fulfilling life, thanks to meditation, which has taught me to accept life as it is. I have developed faith in a mysterious power that is God. Of the many values I have learned from my parents, this one stands out.

Story 42

The Value of Giving from the Heart

By Veha Vig

During the COVID-19 pandemic, I was travelling from Boston to Bangalore after being away for two years. I was stuck in Mumbai, about a thousand kilometers from home, on a stationary bus for over 11 hours without food, water, local currency, or a local sim-card.

My father contacted friends in Mumbai and ensured I was as comfortable as anyone could be in that situation. After 22 hours by road, I reached Belgam which is 300.7 miles and my loving father picked me up, and we reached home to Bangalore after another 8.26 hours by road. It was a tiring experience, and I was grateful to be with my family.

My father was concerned how the underprivileged communities would manage to feed their families with the lockdown and job layoffs. He raised money for meals, biscuits, juice, and chocolates for families and children living in poverty-stricken areas within the Bangalore locality. His friends often asked why he spent long hours outside, risking his health and safety. He said he wished he could do more, and his services felt like a drop in the ocean.

My father was motivated by his belief that humans need a soul filled with love and willing hands to help others in distress. When I joined him for these food runs, I realized that this little drop of water in the ocean mattered significantly to those who needed these services. These small acts of kindness multiplied by a thousand, helped transform our city and provide comfort to the migrant workers in these difficult times.

One day, my parents and volunteers from the community visited a cow shelter to feed the cows. They saw hundreds of migrant workers walking, some bare feet, towards the airport—determined to reach their homes. Shocked, my parents packed and distributed about a hundred food kits the next day. The kits were over in less than three minutes.

Over the next month, over 28 volunteers under my father's able leadership packed around a thousand non-perishable kits of food, sanitary goods for women and dental care products in our home. We received requests for help from nursing homes, orphanages, blind schools, the disabled, and pregnant women.

I have been humbled watching my father take charge of the situation, act without hesitation, and serve people with love, warmth, and a beautiful smile. I believe I came home during the pandemic to experience how to serve the needy compassionately, to become a strong leader, and a good human being.

My parents believe that what you give to the universe, the universe will give back to you profusely. Serving altruistically has brought my parents an abundance of love, respect, cheer, and warmth from our society, friends, and family from around the world.

I am confident the universe will give back to my father in manifold ways, as he continues to do God's work by serving the deprived.

Story 43

In Giving We Receive

By Chandra Akkhial

When I was in primary school, I helped several of my classmates and younger friends from my village in various subjects, especially math. Most of them were from modest homes.

After I passed the exam that qualified me to receive a scholarship, I attended high school in a nearby city. Three of my friends who were academically capable were not able to continue their studies as their parents could not afford financially to send them to high school. I spoke to their parents and offered to pay their fees, and thus convinced them to allow my friends to attend high school. I was able to do this from my scholarship money and tuition earnings. We also convinced the high school principal to give to these three friends some free concessions.

My friends got their high school diploma, and I was incredibly happy. Initially, my parents were not happy about my socializing with the three friends, as they all belonged to minority communities, especially Manohar, who was from the untouchable (Harijan) community.

Manohar got a part-time clerical job in the same high school and later finished his B.A. degree and became a high school teacher. Satyappa, who belonged to a Scheduled (minority) Caste, became a police constable. Hussain, a Muslim, who we called Appa Saheb, was a little more entrepreneurial and ventured to come to Bombay (now Mumbai) when I had joined the Bombay School of Economics for my Master's Degree. He took additional training in Accounting and got a good job in an attorney's office. Now, Hussain's son Ashraf, a talented young man, is a successful software engineer.

I have good memories of my three friends, and often think how I was instrumental in making a change in their lives and the lives of their children. I feel happy and thank the Lord for giving me the good sense to help my friends when I was just making my ends meet.

Often, during those times, there were days when at the end of the month, I had no money; not even for movies or visits to restaurants. But I didn't feel deprived.

I was happy then, and I am happier now. I am not sure if I am as much of a giver now as I was then.

Story 44

The Joy of a Well-Connected Family

By Kimberly Valentour

From my parents, I learned the value of sticking together through good and bad, happy and difficult times. I have four brothers and sisters, and we never think twice if someone needs our help or support.

For example, my husband John was diagnosed with cancer in March 2018. He was undergoing treatments for many months. He and I had ridden in Pelotonia—an annual bike ride fundraiser—to raise money for the James Hospital with the goal of curing cancer. My husband had ridden the previous three to four years but not that year. I almost cancelled my participation, but then I thought to myself, *Why would I do that?* I needed to ride! So, I invited my son Frank to ride with me, and he agreed without hesitation. When people knew I was riding, they donated to my fundraiser without even being asked.

The biggest surprise was on the day of the ride. John was well enough to go to Columbus with me and attend the dinner the evening before the ride. He was going to meet me and Frank at the end of the ride, so we wouldn't have to ride the bus back.

When Frank and I crossed the finish line, I was shocked to see my brothers, sisters, and all their spouses waiting with John to greet us. They were cheering and clapping for us, all smiles. All I could do was cry. I had no idea they were going to be there when we finished.

I have never felt so much love before.

Story 45

Kindness Has No Limits

By Kimberly Valentour

When I was 6 or 7 years old, my father was laid off from his job. My mother did not work outside the home, so she could take care of the five children and manage the house. My parents were very frugal. We had many relatives living nearby who were more than willing to help us when needed. There was also a small country store down the road owned by a Miss Michaels. She sold groceries and household supplies.

One day, she called our house and said that one of my brothers had forgotten something when he was there to buy some milk. So, my mom sent my brother back to the store to pick up whatever it was he had forgotten. He came back carrying a bag full of groceries. Miss Michaels had picked out food for us that she knew we could not afford. She knew what was going on in the neighborhood, and I am sure she helped others out, too.

I think this was also a way of giving us something without making my parents feel embarrassed.

Story 16

The Value of Effective Action

By Nazareth K

The year was 1982. I was working for the Indian Postal system in Southern India and needed to make a trip to inspect the Manakpur Branch Post Office in the state of Karnataka. To reach Manakpur, I had to travel by bus, which left from the Ichalkaranji government bus stop in Maharashtra.

According to the rules of the bus stand, only those with tickets could board the bus and sit in numbered seats. I purchased my ticket and boarded the bus along with other passengers. But there was no empty seat. As I stood, the conductor noticed that four other passengers were also standing. He checked his sheet and asked passengers without tickets to raise their hands. Five people raised their hands.

The conductor went to them, took the money for the tickets, but kept the tickets. He asked the five to wait by the exit door and followed them. He gave the bus driver a signal to stop in the middle of a bridge and asked the five passengers to get down. They asked why.

"You are government employees and have violated the rules. You entered the bus without tickets," he said.

He warned them that if they delayed the bus further, they would be taken to the police station, where a case would be filed against them for violating the rules. The five men got down, and the bus proceeded to its destination.

This act of the conductor surprised me.

I asked him, "Why did you do this?"

He said, "They are educated, and so are you. You bought a ticket and boarded the bus. They did not. They will have to walk about four kilometers to catch a bus. It is a punishment they will not forget. To file a police case would cause delay to the other passengers and for the case to get through, a year."

I was impressed by the action of the bus conductor and felt it was an effective way of enforcing government rules by government employees.

Story 49

My Father's Story

By Rishi Badhwar

My father died on August 28, 2018. On the day of his death anniversary, I was thinking about him and reminiscing about the time I spent with him. I remembered one of his stories, when I was in high school, that he had shared with me.

My father, Mr. Satinder Kumar Badhwar was the oldest son of a family of five. My grandfather, Mr. Inderjeet Badhwar, was Deputy Chief Inspector of Mines and a renowned mining engineer in the Office of the Department of Mines of the Government of India. In those days, all mining in India was private, and the mines were British and Indian owned. Even after independence in 1947, the mines continued to be private, and it was almost 25 years later that they were nationalized.

My grandfather lived in a nice bungalow provided by the government along with a Jeep and a personal peon (attendant) cum driver to drive him to various coal mines. One day, while the driver was waiting under the car porch for my grandfather, my father sneakily approached him and asked him to teach him to drive. At first, the driver was hesitant but then decided to just give my father a few basic lessons on various car parts such as brakes, gears etc.

Every day, my father would get his lesson from the driver.

One day, my father asked the driver to let him hold the steering wheel while the driver sat on the seat and had full control of brakes and gears, etc. This continued till my father asked to change gears while the driver was driving inside the grounds of the bungalow. Soon, my father started driving the car around the bungalow and asking the driver to disconnect the mileage record on the Jeep, so my grandfather would not notice the mileage and reprimand the driver.

The Jeep was given to my grandfather for official use, which meant only while he was on work. One day while my father was driving, my grandfather came out of the house and saw what was going on. He was pleased that his son was learning to drive by a trained and reliable man.

My grandfather bought another car for the use of the family. My father used to drive this car to high school and did some errands for the house, too. He really enjoyed driving that car. When he was telling me this story, I could see how it perked him up. He really loved cars.

Story 50

A "Can Do" Attitude Goes a Long Way

By Alice Bradfield

Growing up, our experiences help to shape what we become as adults. Two little moments from my childhood, which got me on the path to approaching challenges with confidence, stand out.

When I was a child, there was little money to go around, and my parents worked continually to stretch the family's dollars. They were frugal and inventive.

My mother, for example, was a self-taught seamstress. One day, when she was sewing a dress, she accidentally cut the front of the fabric, near the bottom. It was a plain fabric, so there was no way to hide the cut. Or was there? My mother soon figured out what to do. She sewed a colorful, contrasting patch over the cut and added a collar and cuffs to match the patch. I was extremely impressed and have many fond memories of my resourceful mother. I remember this incident when I look at the photographs of her in that dress.

Similarly, my father showed self confidence in solving problems he encountered. One day, I went into the kitchen and found him taking the oven door apart. The door-spring had broken, so the door dropped down and stayed open. I watched my father as he figured out how to fix the door. He took it apart, systematically laying the parts aside, so he did not lose sight of their order.

As he worked, I asked, "How do you know how to fix the door?"

My father answered honestly, "I don't, but I have the confidence that I can figure it out."

And, of course, with an attitude like that, he soon had the door repaired.

My parents modeled life lessons through many small situations. Collectively, those lessons had a profound effect on me.

And so, I adopted the "Can Do" attitude that was modeled for me. I try to approach challenges with the confidence that I can figure them out, whether it is fixing something or stretching money to go further than it wants to. Using one's well spring of inner confidence, systematically "taking things apart" and putting them together again, fixes many things and situations.

As a parent, I have tried to remember the adage: "Your children are watching." As a child, I certainly was!

Story 51

The Lesson in a Mother's Anger

By Rashmi Luthra

When I was seven years old, my father took a job with the Asian Development Bank in Manila, Philippines. I had to leave my school in Delhi in India and my familiar surroundings. Suddenly, I also had an adopted brother, almost my own age, who came along with us. I was hurt that my mother was now paying attention to someone other than myself.

During our first morning in Manila in a rented apartment, my mother served breakfast to my newly adopted brother before serving me. In retaliation, I started fussing and being mean to my brother in my own childish way, complaining about the intrusion in my life. My mother scolded me and sent me to my room without breakfast.

After a while she came to my room, gently pulled me close and with a kind but firm voice explained to me that because my brother was far away from his birth family, we all had to go out of our way to make him feel at home. That is why he was getting an extra share of attention.

It took me some time to fully absorb her message, but her gentle and loving manner and her constant affection for me reassured me that there was love enough for everyone. That one act of a mother so constant in her love and so devoted to her principles grew into a lifelong lesson that we must look beyond our immediate suffering to have compassion for another.

I hope I have passed this message to my children and that my daughter will now pass along this message to her daughter.

Story 52

The Legacy of a Father's Kindness

By Rashmi Luthra

My father made many kind gestures in his life. However, one particular one has stood out for me.

Relatively newly married, he discovered that his sister, recently widowed, was being ill-treated by her in-laws. He decided that she and her three children must leave immediately and live with him. He and my mother gave great affection to the children, and to this day, the bonds of affection are unbreakable.

Many years later, one of those nieces, recently widowed at the age of 48 and with a son in his twenties studying to be a doctor, was detected with ovarian cancer. The son, having just lost his father to a heart attack, now faced the prospect of losing his mother a few months later. My father moved to New York to be with the young man and stayed until his niece's death, so that her son would not have to face her departure alone.

My father never learned to cook, depending on my mother for his daily needs. However, in those days in New York, he somehow figured out how to make carrot pudding for my nephew. He apologized ahead, saying it would never be as good as my mother's. My nephew in turn joked that it might have superseded my mom's carrot pudding. In this way, at a very dark time, the tenderness of such moments provided solace.

While these are small gestures, when put together, represent life's very purpose. That purpose, as my father taught me, is about dropping everything to hold the hand of a loved one in need.

Part Two
Other Stories

Introduction to Part Two

This part includes stories of individuals who have struggled in their lives and yet emerged victorious and successful. I have collected these from newspapers, magazines, books, and quotes.

I want to give readers a glimpse of the variety of inspirational stories from different strata of society. The biographies and achievements of the rich and famous in business, science, art and entertainment, inventions, academia, medicine, and culinary art are not uncommon.

However, there is not much attention to and coverage of the success stories of ordinary people from humble beginnings. These could be homemakers, students, children of poor families and farmers—people who are not famous but achieved success in their lives due to their determination, perseverance, faith and hope, and inspiration from their elders. In my research, I found such stories in newspapers and magazines.

I am also presenting profiles of celebrities who faced challenges—unhappy marriages, poverty, rejections from universities of their dreams, or those who had no idea about their talent that allowed them to succeed. Many of them came from poor families and had much struggle. They were immigrants or those who lost everything in a war or the Depression and had no money or skills. It was perseverance, faith in themselves, devotion, hope, and inspiration that led them to the top of the ladder of success.

Section A features a peace activist and organic farmer from Athens Ohio; two Indian men who have excelled in their studies, one who was a medical student convicted of murder and the other from a poor farming family; a valedictorian in a U.S. college who was once homeless; and the institution Big Brothers Big Sisters in the U.S.

Section B features Indian women who have overcome fear by taking risks and not allowing their socialization to hold them back. I found these in a supplement of the Indian national daily, the *Times of India* (TOI), which every year pays tribute to women on Women's Day, March 8. As a part of this section, there are short profiles of businesswomen who have taken great risk and overcome fear of failure.

Section C features a well-known actor, who values family life and was inspired by his father; a successful chef who had not cooked in her life till she was 34 years old; and a millionaire writer and philanthropist, who faced extreme poverty and depression, but rose above it.

Section D is a homage to two very well known and courageous women, a wildlife specialist and a lawyer, both who overcame all stereotypes and were recognized for their work and success. However, at every step of the way they faced discrimination and ridicule.

Section A

FROM THE ORDINARY TO THE EXTRAORDINARY

Art Gish: Life is Precious

"We buy the things we do not need to impress the people we do not like."

In every community, there are role models that inspire us to be better than we are. Art Gish is one such example. I was fortunate to know him and his wife Peggy, not as friends, but as concerned community members of the town I live in.

Living in Athens, one could not miss Art and Peggy. My husband Raj and I were frequent visitors to the local Farmer's Market where the Gishes had a prominent stall, full of fresh local vegetables and an abundance of Asian vegetables from India, Thailand, and China. International students and faculty at Ohio University flocked to his stall, which was the only one offering these vegetables and in such a variety. He was eager to learn how to grow these vegetables better and how we cooked them. He had many questions when people visited his stall and chatted with members of the international community.

It was on these days that we, at innumerable times, discussed the life of Gandhi and other leaders of India who were world figures in promoting non-violent movements. Later we also saw Art and Peggy with a few others, in front of the Athens Courthouse protesting peacefully, with banners about U.S. government's policies and war and aggression.

Arthur G. Gish, as was his full name, was a peace activist, preacher, writer, and public speaker. He was known for his opposition to a number of conflicts, ranging from the Vietnam War to the Iraq War. He died in 2010 in an accident on his farm in Athens county, when his tractor rolled back onto him.

Gish was born and raised on a farm in Lancaster County, Pennsylvania, and held degrees from Manchester College in North Manchester, Indiana, and Bethany Theological Seminary.

Gish and his wife, Peggy, were organic farmers and life-long peace workers. The Gishes were members of the New Covenant Fellowship in

Athens, Ohio, a communal church affiliated with the Church of the Brethren. As a church member, Art was greatly respected.

At his death, Stan Noffsinger, the church's general secretary, said, "We have lost a person important to the Church of the Brethren who has been a visible witness to Christ's peace around the world. It is a true loss to the church and the thousands remembering Gish's strong witness for active Christian peacemaking of people he served. We mourn this loss."

Gish's peacemaking career began as a conscientious objector working in Europe through Brethren Volunteer Service (BVS) in the years 1958-1960. According to a biographical note in "Hebron Journal," Gish "opposed United States involvement in every war since his youth." He is remembered for his participation in the Civil Rights movement of the 1960s and the anti-war movement of the 1970s, and for his work for peace in the Middle East in more recent decades.

An interview in the magazine *The Messenger* of August 13, 1970, described him as an author of several books, a speaker, and preacher with "incisive and frequently controversial views," as characterized in his church and peace movement circles, including The New Left and Christian Radicalism.

In an interview, Gish said, "Working in the protest movement, I have come to see that the early Brethren and the Anabaptists were not conservatives. They were the radicals of their day. The early Brethren understood that a Christian is different from the world, that a Christian stands against the world and is in conflict with the world. To be at peace with God means that one is in conflict with the world."

The Athens News in his obituary wrote, "On a regular basis, one or both of the Gishes could be found with a few other people standing on Court Street outside the Athens County Courthouse, holding signs calling for peace, in a weekly lunch hour vigil." Art Gish also was placed first in the reader-nominated Athens News Best of Athens awards, as "Best Leading Citizen," the newspaper reported.

Rich Tomsu, also an organic farmer in Athens, admired Gish's knowledge of world history, politics, agriculture, environmental science, and religion and said, "Art embraced the totality of life with joy." He wrote about Gish's staunch belief in universal brotherhood, justice, respect for all religions and all human beings, and opposition to wars and violence. He was a true believer in world peace. "He prayed alongside Muslims and Jews and went to Church regularly."

Art's outstanding trait that appealed to me was the way he inspired people around him to develop a positive outlook on life. People were charmed by his favorite phrase, "It is a great day to be alive," which brought joy to people around him. In summer, winter, rain, storm, or sunshine, he would greet people with this phrase and a smile.

In Rich's words, "Art was the conscience of our community. He possessed the fine qualities of humanity that we all try to achieve and wish to possess—qualities of compassion, intellectual curiosity, courage, honesty, optimism, tolerance, and an unquenchable thirst for justice. Art taught me a simple but often neglected truth—life is precious."

I am touched by Art Gish's approach to life as well as his idea that "life is precious." He lived his faith and practiced what he preached.

Anurag Tewari: Who Inspired Who, Father or Son?
"The motivation to dream big came from my hard-working parents."

This is a story of a young man whose father, a farmer, could not dream of sending his son for higher education. But his outstanding academic performance took him to Cornell University, an Ivy League school in the U.S.

According to the national daily, *Times of India*, Anurag Tewari made headlines in Indian newspapers. A son of a farmer Kamalapati Tewari and homemaker Sangeeta Tewari, Anurag till Class V, attended a primary school in his village, Sarasan, 60 kilometers from Lakhimpur town which is 2172 miles from Bangalore city, Karnataka state, India.

In Class VI, he qualified for the entrance test to Vidya Gyan, a rural leadership academy in Sitapur which is 2119 km or 1316.7 miles by road from Bangalore city. This academy handpicks economically underprivileged meritorious students from rural Uttar Pradesh, the state in north India.

"The call letter in 2013 changed my life. The motivation to dream big, came from my hard-working parents. Support came from my three sisters, who wanted me to get the world class education they couldn't," said Anurag.

According to the *Times of India* article, Anurag scored 1370 out of 1600 (86.7), in his SAT exam. He applied to Cornell University, U.S., as an "Early Decision Applicant" or in the "Early Admission Program" as termed in the U.S. His schoolteachers helped him in writing and editing his essays for Cornell's Early Admission Program and his counsellors at Delhi, helped in selecting colleges. He received the call for his admission to Cornell in December 2019. He decided to study humanities, and in his interview to TOI, Anurag said, "This decision was questioned by many who felt it was not suitable for boys."

Anurag's efforts and achievements can be more appreciated when one looks at his circumstances and environment. Till just four years ago, Anurag's village did not even have electricity. A humanities student, Anurag scored a perfect 100 in economics and history, 99 in political science, and 97 in English, but 95 in mathematics. Anurag started the fall semester in 2020, taking online courses in economics and mathematics at Cornell.

"When I reached my village after class XII, everyone looked at me with high regard. People who did not know me earlier came to my house just to talk to me. It gives me happiness," said Anurag. The *Times* reported that, "Anurag finds inspiration in ace cricketer M.S. Dhoni." Dhoni is India's famous Wicketkeeper—Batsman and is internationally known figure in the world of Cricket.

Now, after Anurag's acceptance at Cornell and his popularity, the father says, "I thought of making my son successful, but today, he has made me a successful father. He taught me so much in all these years."

It is hard to say who motivated who, but it is clear that motivation is an infectious trait. And, at the end of the day, it does not matter who motivates who. It is a joint victory.

Subhash Patil: From Murderer to Doctor
"I spent a lot of time in the jail library and never lost interest in studies."

Could a murderer motivate you? In life, on the spur of the moment, a mistake could be made, or a crime committed. To rectify it and to continue on the path prior to the incident is a real challenge. These acts of heroism are an example and source of motivation for others. Such stories are rare, and that is why it finds a place here.

In 2002, Subhash Tukaram Patil, a medical student, got a life sentence for murdering his lover's husband. He was incarcerated in the Central Jail of Bangalore, in the southern state of Karnataka in India.

The national daily, *Times of India* (TOI), reported that Patil "was in love with a married woman and abetted by her, he shot and killed her husband, an excise contractor."

"I was jailed when I was doing my MBBS (Bachelor of Medicine, Bachelor of Surgery) at the Hyderabad Education Society's Mahadeveppa Rampure Medical College (MRMC) in Kalaburagi. In prison, I worked in the jail's Outpatient Department (OPD)," says Patil. Kalaburagi or Gulbarga is a city in the Indian state of Karnataka.

In 2016, he was released for good conduct and picked up his medical studies where he left off, graduating in 2019. He received his MBBS degree at the convocation on February 15, 2020. He has been doing his Residency since 2019 at Basaveshwar Hospital, in Gulbarga.

"I am committed to serving society, especially relatives of prisoners and soldiers. I spent a lot of time in the jail library and never lost interest in studies," says Patil. The TOI article reported that Patil completed a Karnataka State Open University course in journalism.

One of Patil's classmates, Dr. Kiran Patil, an Ear Nose and Throat (ENT) specialist at Basaveswar Hospital and lecturer at MRMC said they were both classmates in 2002, and it's remarkable that Tewari completed his medical degree after prison. The Dean of MRMC Mr. Umesh Chandra said that though Patil was about 14 years older than his classmates, he completed the course successfully.

This story is inspiring as it tells of a young man from a village who had a purpose in life. The crime he committed and his good behavior in prison were an impetus to do better when he was released and complete his education.

Megan Faircloth: Valedictorian who was once Homeless
"We did not have much money for food or anything either."

I read this story and wondered: *How is this possible?* I wanted to share it.

Megan Faircloth from Wendell, Wake County, North Carolina in the U.S., in her graduation speech said that for most of her junior year and early senior year of high school, she and her family were homeless. While other students waited anxiously to find out where they would be accepted to college, Megan did not know where she would sleep at night, reported *The Athens Messenger*, the local newspaper of Athens, Ohio.

"At one point, we were in a homeless shelter. Then we were staying with relatives for a while, and then we lived in a car," said the 17-year-old Megan. Her family was evicted from their original home at Wendell in November 2015, and since then, it had been a struggle for the entire Faircloth family of four.

"We'd be running around all day and then we'd get a motel room at 12 o'clock at night. It's then I'd have to start my homework," Megan said. "It was physically exhausting. We did not have much money for food or anything either."

When they did not have money for a motel, Megan, her two siblings and her mother would sleep in their car, seeking parking areas that would be safe. Their car windows were jammed and would not roll up.

In winter, "It was really cold and then when it started warming up, it got really hot," said Megan. In July 2016, they moved to one of her sibling's houses, but were evicted from there, too. In October 2017, they moved to a house in Wendell, where they live now.

Megan graduated at the top of her class with a 5.25 GPA. She was struggling with her seven advanced placement classes but determined that her grades should not slip. She did not have a return address for her college application. She received a near full scholarship to Stanford University, a top Ivy League school of in the U.S.

"She persevered through the adversity to achieve the highest-class rank," according to *The Athens Messenger*.

Melba, Megan's mother, says, "Homelessness was horrible. But when you hit rock bottom, the only place you can go is up, right?" Megan described her daughter as, "Tough. I think she can do anything she wanted to do. She has a lot of determination, and a lot of people would have given up but not she. She is a fighter. She has always been a fighter."

After Megan's address at the banquet at the commencement ceremony, getting off the stage, she said, "I looked around at the audience and everybody was standing and clapping. Oh my God, I did not think what I said would have that much effect on people."

Afterwards, many students came up to her and said that her speech had inspired them.

According to the *Messenger*, more than 50 students at East Wake are homeless. The authorities are collecting items of need and have a food pantry for the needy.

Megan struggled a great deal but was determined and never gave up. What was her inspiration? Megan says it was *Unbroken*, the story of Olympic track star Louis Zamperini, who survived 47 days on a raft at sea after a plane crash and spent more than two years as a prisoner of war during World War II.

Big Brothers, Big Sisters (BBBS): Building Networks of Care

There are many on the margins of society. Where do they go? Fortunately, there are organizations working with and for them. One such organization is Big Brothers, Big Sisters (BBBS), which motivates young people through mentoring programs.

The story of the Mentoring Program of BBBS triggered memories of my undergraduate days in Patna, India, in a women's college managed by Catholic nuns. The college offered boarding and lodging called hostels, where students could stay. There was strict discipline and there were rules and routines for everything—study hours, cafeteria, outdoor sports, and bedtime.

Final year students mentored the newcomers and residents of the hostel. Without TV, internet, computers, or cell phones, the only entertainment was going to the movies, shopping, or eating in restaurants. We were allowed out for fixed hours at a time, and the college buses dropped us off and picked us up. There was companionship and good conversation about our personal lives, and we enjoyed each other's company. The seniors were motivated to be leaders and role models and the juniors felt comfortable and cared for. In BBBS program of U.S.A. also, there is matching of the mentors and school children, just like the Patna program of matching seniors to juniors.

The BBBS of America, according to their website, is the oldest and largest youth mentoring organization in the United States since 1904. The 240 agencies across the country operate in all 50 states and serve youth from age of five years into young adulthood in both community-based and site-based settings.

The programs match elementary school children, known as "Littles," with high school kids, the "Bigs," based on their interests and personalities. This matching is to provide empathy, support, and attention for the younger counterparts at school, whether they are adjusting to a new school, transitioning to another grade, or struggling to connect with their peers. More than 400,000 Littles, their families, their Bigs, and other mission-critical volunteers are part of evidence-based mentoring.

During this process, Littles experience the positive power of peers, and the Bigs develop self-esteem and pride that they are role models, show empathy, moral reasoning, and communication skills.

Marcus Whitman, counselor of the high school in Rushville, NY, says, "It is for kids who are not picked for athletics or the school play. Just because they are not chosen, does not mean they do not have tremendous gifts to offer. The program is also ideal for kids whose families are not able to enroll them in extracurricular activities or programs outside schools. It is beneficial for those kids who are not interested in such activities. When I invite a student to be part of High School Bigs program, many act as if they have won a lottery."

Ashlee Thorton, who graduated from the Marcus Whitman High School as a Little, says that her three years in this program helped her to overcome her shyness.

"If I hadn't done the program when I was little, I wouldn't know how to cope, and I wouldn't have anyone to talk to." She worked as a Big during her final three years of high School. "I have someone looking up to me and it is an amazing feeling."

There are huge benefits of the programs. The Littles say they get better grades, improved attendance in school, and a positive outlook for the future. The Bigs say have more self-esteem; more stepping out of their comfort zones, setting, and striving for higher goals, more likely to be involved in the community, and "I know someone is learning and watching and that is a great feeling."

Both Bigs and Littles say relationships are more intense, the world makes sense, and there is a change in their outlook. The BBBS has an amazing record. Some highlights:

- In 2019, some 135,786 Littles were served by the BBBS network.
- The community-based matches, in the last 31 months, over 35 percent lasted longer than the average match length 10 years ago.
- The community-based matches surveyed in 2019 made significant improvements from baseline to follow-up in all eight outcomes areas: parental trust, attitudes towards risky behaviors, grades, educational expectations, school attendance (new measurement area), ability to get along with peers (social competence), juvenile justice involvement, and the presence of a special adult.
- After at least a year of mentoring, over 95 percent of community-based and over 89 percent of site-based Littles report that they feel they have a special adult in their life.

The BBBS programs offer a hand to young people who do not fit perfectly into the school system or society. At the same time, it identifies and encourages young adults to reach out to these younger people and mentor them. It is a wonderful exchange of energy, interest, empathy, and care.

Section B

WOMEN WHO MADE IT: FROM FEAR TO FEARLESSNESS

This section offers stories selected from an insert in the national daily, *The Times of India* (TOI) on Fearlessness called LIFE, a special edition for International Women's Day 2020. The women profiled are mostly from ordinary walks of life and have overcome fear.

The insert opens with a definition of fear: "Fear is a four-letter word that confronts all of us. As a child, you fear heights. As a grown-up, you fear failure. And as a woman, you are conditioned to fear everything."

But today, women are facing their fear boldly and speak openly about the ways to conquer it.

Ankiti Bose: Co-Founder, Zilingo

"Failure is never the end but an opportunity to learn.
Fight the fear. In this case the fear of failure."

Bose is the first Indian woman CEO of a high valued startup just short of the 1 billion mark. According to *Forbes* magazine, "Ankiti quit her job before her 24th birthday to set up Zilingo."

A technology and commerce platform in the fashion industry, Zilingo has its headquarters in Singapore. It started in 2015, co-founded by Ankiti Bose and Dhruv Kapoor and operates in Indonesia, Hong Kong, Thailand, Philippines, Australia, India, and the United States. It started with 500 employees. Zilingo means the "Gift of God."

Describing her success, Bose says, "The journey towards greatness is laced with sacrifice. Some sacrifices we pre-empt, some we are happy to make, and some creep in. The vision for what we wanted to make at Zilingo meant working around the clock, traveling like a vagabond, and not a shoulder to cry on."

Bose says these are scary emotions, but we prevail when we channel our fears into empathy and trust our instincts and passion to guide us.

"Forgive people, grow a thick skin, and navigate with confidence and empathy—not fear or anger. The journey can be lonely, and people may leave you, so get comfortable with solitude and the possibility of failure."

Monika Mahendra Singh:
Founder and President of Mahendra Singh Foundation

"Be it India or New York, it is a struggle everywhere.
What is important is to act and emerge from your struggles
and not rely on others for help.
I believe a woman who understands the power of her own voice is fearless."

In 2005, 18-year-old Singh was visiting her hometown Lucknow, India. Riding in a car, she rolled her window down and was attacked by men who threw acid on her face and body. Singh says the attackers were hired by a man who wanted to punish her for refusing his marriage proposal.

She spent nine years in and out of hospital. "I lived in trauma in the ICU for years. But I do not allow myself to relive those days. Now others see me as a professional. I have no fear of getting hurt, physically," she says.

Since she was a child, Singh dreamed of being a fashion designer. She enrolled at the National Institute of Design in New Delhi and was in her first year when the acid incident happened. She completed her fashion design course and was accepted at the Parsons School of Design in New York.

Singh established her dream project, the Mahendra Singh Foundation. Named after her deceased father to whom she says she owes everything in life, Singh aims to generate awareness and support victims of rape, acid attacks, and other violent crimes. Singh and the Foundation are based in New York. She is also associated with and Vice President of Make Love Not Scars (MLNS), an NGO based out of New Delhi.

Nayantara Jain: Scuba Diver to Conservationist

"But being fearless is knowing it, fighting it and getting over it.
Do not get over-powered by fear. But conquer it. Become fearless.

Jain was a philosophy major when she decided to become a conservationist and applied for and got admission to the Marine Biology and Conservation course in San Diego, U.S.A. She was afraid, as she had not studied science.

"I got over it by maintaining focus on the larger goal: to work in conservation," says Jain.

During her coursework, she learned to ask for help. "People are really helpful in the actual world, more than we think." A lesson she learned and wants to share is for parents not to set too many conditions and expectations from their children while growing up. "Tell them that in life you can be anything, and you don't have to be everything."

Jain has been running her own organization for six years. Her goal is to raise more confident and fearless women as role models. Jain believes that there is nothing like no fear; fear will always be there.

Shailja Mittal: Founder, Koala Kabs
"Fearlessness provides us with inner strength to fight fear.
It makes you confident and strong to fight every odd and stand like a rock by every decision you take.
To build rock-like attitude, one needs inspiration too."

Shailja Mittal and Anmol Gupta started Koala Kabs in 2017. A cab service for women, run by women, it was born out of a mother's instinct to ensure the safety of her daughter. A fleet of 15 cabs in the Delhi NCR area offers reliable and safe transport for women to travel to and from their workplace, college, and other activities and for children to go to school.

The service empowers women drivers by giving them control of the car they drive and the responsibility to protect their passengers. It caters to children and senior citizens and has a strict "no male passengers in the age group of 18-60 years" policy. Named after Koala Bears, who are cute and harmless but are very ferocious when it comes to protecting their young, Koala Kabs is a great initiative for women, children, and senior citizens.

Mittal's experience stresses the importance of overcoming fear and being inspired, two elements essential for achieving your goals. Mittal says she found a sea of inspiration in her mother.

"I learned how to balance work and personal life and manage adversities from her," says Mittal.

**Asma Khan: First British Chef to be Featured in
the Popular Series *Chef's Table* in London**
*"When one lets one's faith take over the mind,
one turns fearless because it is your faith that will say,
'it will be ok if we overcome the fear'.
Every time I see a hurdle, I know I will not hit the hurdle.
I visualize not just clearing the hurdle but flying over it."*

Asma Khan is an Indian-born British chef, restaurateur, and cookbook author. She owns the Darjeeling Express restaurant in London's Soho and was profiled on the sixth season of the documentary series *Chef's Table*. In June 2019, *Business Insider* named her number 1 on their list of "100 Coolest People in Food and Drink."

Although Asma loved food, she left home without ever learning to cook. When she married and moved to Cambridge to join her husband in 1991, she could not even boil an egg. Separated from home and unable to recreate the food she loved and missed, she felt isolated and alone. Determined to learn how to cook, she returned to India for a few months and busied herself in the kitchens of her home, where she learned to craft the royal Mughlai dishes of her childhood from the household cooks, as well as from her mother and mother-in-law.

Returning to the UK, she had two children, became the first woman in her family to attend college, qualified as a lawyer, and completed a doctorate in British Constitutional Law at King's College, London.

"My father still calls me 'Doctor Asma,'" she laughs.

But her heart lay in cooking. She started a supper club, and eventually, the restaurant Darjeeling Express. Khan's brigade is made up entirely of women—many of whom are second generation daughters and immigrants—who cook and serve Asma's dishes with warmth and love. "We all cook with the desire to embrace someone," she says. "We're not cooking to make money. We're cooking because we all know what it is to be without family, without the comfort of having your own food."

Asma credits her father for her attitude of becoming fearless. "I have a PhD, but my real education was listening to my father," she says.

WOMEN WHO HAVE EXCELED IN THEIR BUSINESSES
In India, it is not easy for women to excel in business. However, this is changing, and more women are coming into the field and starting their businesses, taking risks, and overcoming fear.

Neha Kant co-founded a company known as Clovia for redefining the Indian lingerie market; Ayushi Gudwani started a company to make workwear fit every Indian body type and Alankrita Shrivastav, a filmmaker, fought for her space to tell stories. All these women say 'fear' is the greatest hurdle to progress.

Neha Kant: When Kant was forming her company, she was pregnant and worried that her parental responsibilities would interfere with her new business.

"I decided to treat this as another responsibility and once I took the plunge, magic happened," says Neha. "Today both my son and my business are flourishing. Once you push yourself, magic happens."

Ayushi Gudwani: Gudwani describes her two prominent fears: stage fright as a child and fear of failure when starting her new company, Fable Street. As a child, she forced herself to go on stage and told herself that if she messes up and fumbles few times, it will be okay at the end. As an entrepreneur, she was afraid of the risk but decided to go for the "Mindset Shift." She told herself, "After 40 years when I look back would I rather tell myself that I tried but failed rather than saying, I lost the opportunity." What a wonderful attitude to life!

Alankrita Shrivastava: When Shrivastava was 19 years old, both her parents were seriously ill. Her mother was diagnosed with cancer, and her father was quite ill too. Her biggest fear was losing her parents. She took on more responsibilities, besides taking care of her parents, and this helped her in becoming strong. She was fearful about the future. Her Buddhist practice helped her in coping with fear.

"The fear that my parents will not be around, the feeling of living in constant dread, toughened me," says Srivastava. During this journey, she was determined to complete her film work and complete it "by hook or crook." As she says, "Fearlessness is the courage of conviction."

Section 6

ON BECOMING A CELEBRITY

In my introduction to this section of the book, I wrote there are luminaries or celebrities who faced challenges, such as poverty, war, migration, or were in dysfunctional families and had no tradable skills. Such persons need to be recognized and commended as it was perseverance, faith in themselves, devotion, hope, and sheer inspiration that led to their success.

Also, many of these felt strongly about ethics, values, and societal codes of conduct. Often successful people forget about these values. In this section, I present the actor Hugh Jackman, the chef and writer Julia Child, and J.K. Rowling, author of the *Harry Potter* series.

Hugh Jackman: A Love for Family Values

"My family has been the greatest blessing in my life. My father has been my rock, and if there are any good qualities about me, I give credit largely to my father."

Jackman is an Australian actor, singer, and producer. While he has many prominent roles to his career, he is probably best known for his performances in in the *X-Men* series for which he holds a Guinness World Record for "the longest career as a live-action Marvel superhero."

He featured in the musical *The Greatest Showman* in 2017 for which he received a Grammy Award for Best Soundtrack Album. He played the role of Jean Valjean in *Les Misérables* and was nominated for the Academy Award for Best Actor in 2013. He won the Golden Globe Award for Best Actor – Motion Pictures, Musical or Comedy. He was appointed a Companion of the Order of Australia in 2019 Queen's Birthday Honors for services to performing arts and to the global community.

But more than anything, Jackman is a family man, devoted to his wife and children.

The Athens Messenger, the local newspaper in my town, on December 23, 2012, had an insert "American Profile," which caught my eye. It was a photograph of Jackman, who was in New York on Father's Day and hosting the Tony Ceremony in June 2012.

He was walking with his children that he called "the greatest blessing of my life." There was also a photograph of his wife Deborra-Lee Furness, and both photographs were captioned, "Jackman Family Values." In this article, Jackman talks about a time in his career when he came home from a tough rehearsal frustrated and said to his wife, "Maybe I am not the right person." (He meant for the role). His wife said to him that if he felt he was not the right person for the part, he would not have been intimidated by this challenge. She urged him to "lose fear, work harder and get in there." This was a lesson in encouragement, overcoming fear, and plunging into the challenge.

Jackman's life shows that he is truly a family man, a devoted husband, and a dedicated parent who strongly believes in family ties and values, the credit of which he gives to his father. In an interview, he says, "My family has been the greatest blessing in my life. My father has been my rock, and if there are any good qualities about me, I give credit largely to my father."

He says his father was a hard worker, humble, and deeply religious, though he does not talk about it. He never said a bad word about anybody. Jackman lost his mother when he was eight years old, and according to him, that "was a time when he (his father), could have gone loose a bit, but he never did."

Jackman and his wife, Furness, both Australians, met in 1995 while working together on a TV show, which was his first professional role as an actor. Furness said the two had an instant connection, and "I feel blessed that I experienced, that I feel like I met my soulmate, whatever that is," she said.

The two married in 1996, a couple years before Jackman became known outside Australia, and have two children. Jackman loves his wife deeply and describes her as completely opposite to him.

"Deb" (her full name is Deborra-Lee Furness) "is the hilarious, fun, sexy, impractical one. I am pragmatic, steady sensible one. When it comes to kids, I am strict and she is lenient," he remarks.

With such contrasts, one would imagine that their marital life would be in turmoil or a sort of an adjustment. But it is not so. On the other hand, it looks like they are made for each other. "Deep down we are very similar," says Jackman. They call each other "10 to 12 times a day" and "do everything together."

"We are madly in love, and it gets more so as it goes on. Most of it finding the right person. When I met my wife, the realization was like a lightning bolt—I knew she was the one for me for the rest of my life."

Jackman's life highlights his good upbringing and a home life reflected in ethical, religious, and moral values.

In today's world, it is rare that a couple says, "we are made for each other" and live a life that exemplifies it.

Julia Child: Never Say Die
"Life itself is a proper binge."

Julia Child was raised in a privileged home and thought cooking "is the job of the staff who prepare and serve you meals." However, when she married, she realized that cooking was an important aspect of running a home. When she and her husband moved to France, she developed an interest in French cooking while watching the cooking channel on TV. Soon, she was taking cooking lessons and experimenting with recipes. Of course, at the back of her mind was the "fear of failure," which was natural.

Soon, Childs was writing books which were translated and marketed all over the world and hosting her own TV show. Who would have expected this? This is the reason I selected her story. It is an inspiration and a motivator.

Childs is one of the leading experts and exponents of French cooking. Her famous cookbook, *Mastering the Art of French Cooking*, made history in the world of French cuisine. From a person used to wealth and luxuries, pampered at home, and knowing nothing about cooking, she shined. Her idea of cooking was of a live-in cook taking orders of one's choice and taste and preparing it. When Childs was on her own and had no help, she ate frozen dinners.

"You don't have to cook fancy or complicated masterpieces—simply good food from fresh ingredients. Find something you are passionate about and keep tremendously interested in it. I was 31 when I started cooking. Up until then, I just ate," she says.

In 1948, two years after she married Paul Cushing Child, an American civil servant and diplomat, he was posted to France. Julia had to set up home, kitchen, and cook. She watched cooking classes on TV and began to try them, discovering she loved French cooking. By 1963, she had mastered the art of French cooking and was confident enough to go on TV, hosting *The French Chef* television series, a popular show from 1963 to 1973.

Imagine a novice in cooking, hosting a TV show after 15 years of her exposure to French cuisine.

In later years, Childs, at the age of 51, and two French women co-authored the cookbook *Mastering the Art of French Cooking*. Her manuscript was rejected by Houghton Mifflin, but Julia never lost hope and persisted with publishers. Eventually, it was accepted by Knopf publishers.

At the age of 55, Childs was diagnosed with breast cancer but recovered quickly. She had a great attitude and said, "I do not want to be a whiny."

Childs wrote and published 30 books. She had many firsts. She was the first woman to be inducted into the National Women's Hall of Fame. She was elected a Fellow of the American Arts and Sciences in 2000 and awarded the U.S. Presidential Medal of Freedom in 2003. She received Honorary Doctorate degrees from Harvard University, Johnson and Wales, Brown and others, including her alma mater, Smith College.

Childs had a great sense of humor and was a very direct person. "The only time to eat diet food is when you are waiting for the steak to get cooked. The only real stumbling block is fear. In cooking, you've got to have a what-the-hell attitude."

She married late, for her times, at the age of 34. The Childs did not have children, as Julia felt it would interfere with her career. She died at the age of 92. Her life is a living example of perseverance, determination, self-belief, confidence, fearlessness, and a lesson of never to lose hope.

J.K. Rowling: You Must Have a Nerve
*"Happiness can be found, even in the darkest of times,
if one only remembers to turn on the light."*

This story of J.K. Rowling is inspirational as it motivates readers to pursue interests and goals with faith and perseverance. In this case, Rowling had an inborn desire to write and a flair for writing. She wrote fantasy drama for young adults, reflected in her *Harry Potter* series.

I chose Rowling's story because she exemplifies another side to being a celebrity—no desire for great riches and not inheriting wealth or status. She had a bad marriage; little or no money; repeated rejects of her submitted manuscripts to publishers. But writing was in her blood. She had no idea that her writing would bring her fortune and be her main livelihood. Her books have fired the imagination of people of all ages.

Joanne Rowling was born in 1965 in Bristol and grew up in England and south-east Wales. Her father, Peter, was an aircraft engineer at the Rolls Royce factory in Bristol and her mother, Anne, was a science technician in the Chemistry department at Joanne's school Wyedean Comprehensive. Anne was diagnosed with multiple sclerosis when Joanne was a teenager and died in 1990, before the *Harry Potter* books were published.

Rowling studied at Exeter University, where she read so widely outside her French and Classics syllabus that she clocked up a fine of £50 for overdue books at the university library. She was at Exeter from 1983 to 1986. Her knowledge of classics would one day come in handy for creating the spells in the *Harry Potter* series, some of which are in Latin. Her course included a year in Paris.

"I lived in Paris for a year as a student," Rowling tweeted after the 2015 terrorist attacks there. "It's one of my favorite places on earth."

After her degree, she moved to London and worked in a series of jobs, including one as a researcher at Amnesty International. "There in my little office I read hastily scribbled letters smuggled out of totalitarian regimes by men and women who were risking imprisonment to inform the outside world of what was happening to them. My small participation in that process was one of the most humbling and inspiring experiences of my life," she said later.

Rowling was passionate about writing from an early age and wrote fantasy stories. While working on her *Harry Potter* series, she wrote whenever and wherever she could and regularly in cafés. As she famously says, "I didn't have to make my own coffee."

According to Goalcast.com, Rowling wrote the first installment of the *Harry Potter* series while her life was at rock bottom. Her mother's death was a traumatic event for her, and her exceptionally short-lived marriage had just collapsed. She was out of work, a single mother battling severe clinical depression—contemplating suicide at one point—and trying to raise a child on state welfare benefits of £68 a week (about US $90 at the time). She was, in her own words, "as poor as it is possible to be in modern Britain, without being homeless," feeling like an epic failure at every level, and living hand to mouth without a hint of a light at the end of the tunnel.

In spite of all her failures and rejections, Rowling never lost hope.

"You sort of start thinking anything's possible if you've got enough nerve," she says.

She was awarded several honorary degrees—from St Andrews University, the University of Edinburgh, Edinburgh Napier University, the University of

Exeter (which she attended), the University of Aberdeen, and Harvard University, where she spoke at the 2008 commencement ceremony.

Her *Harry Potter* novels have sold at least 500 million copies worldwide. The *Harry Potter* movies have grossed more than $7.7 billion. According to *Forbes* magazine, Rowling, in 2020 was the second highest-paid author in the world, behind the prolific James Patterson. She sold nearly 2.6 million books between June 2019 and June 2020. *Harry Potter and the Cursed Child* clocked $2.3 million in ticket sales in a single week, the highest of any non-musical in Broadway's history.

However, books no longer account for most of her earnings: Rowling's biggest cash cow is Universal Studios' "Wizarding World" attractions.

According to her website, in March 2020, J.K. Rowling and Wizarding World partners launched the "Harry Potter at Home" initiative to entertain children locked down at home during the Covid-19 pandemic. It was the first *Harry Potter* book read aloud by celebrities on video and made available free in audiobook and eBook streaming. In May 2020, she announced another initiative to help families in lockdown—*The Ickabog*, a story for younger children serialized for free online, and an accompanying illustration competition.

A book of *The Ickabog*, featuring the winning children's illustrations, was published in November 2020, with the royalties going to charities assisting vulnerable groups affected by the pandemic.

And, according to Goalcast.com, Rowling went from being on welfare to being a multi-millionaire in five years—and perhaps most inspiring is what she has done with her newfound wealth. Rowling never forgot where she came from and donated hundreds of millions of dollars to charities as a result, actively supporting over a dozen organizations, and establishing her own children's foundation, Lumos, in 2005.

Rowling's story is an inspiration and reconfirms that with determination, dedication and hard work pursued with faith, hope and in self-belief, miracles can happen. Anything is possible. It is an inspiration to those who have given up in life.

Section D

TWO FEARLESS WOMEN: BATTLING SEXISM AND DISCRIMINATION

An Ode to Fearless Women
By Nikita Gill
Defined by no man, you are your own story,
blazing through turning history into herstory,
And what they dare to tell you about
All the things you cannot be, you smile and tell them,
"I am both war and woman and you cannot stop me."

I am presenting profiles of two women—Jane Goodall and Ruth Ginsberg—who are famous and well respected. They both came from humble environments, had clear cut goals, and worked with passion and determination. They were smart and probably did not realize that one day they would be outstanding, famous, and get recognition for their work. Interestingly, there are commonalities between these two women.

Both women faced discrimination and unkind remarks from male colleagues and supervisors about their work and achievements, just because they were women. However, this did not deter them in pursuing what they wanted. One wanted to study chimpanzees and the other to achieve top honors in her academic work. Both women were inspired by their mothers, who instilled in them the value of pursuing their dreams.

Goodall's mother joined her in the forests and jungles of Gombe, Tanzania, when she was conducting research. Ginsberg's mother was a pillar of strength and sacrifice, who abandoned her ambition to go to college and chose to save for her children's education in prestigious institutions of higher learning.

Both Goodall and Ginsberg admired their mothers, whom they lost before they became successful. Goodall's mother died the day before she graduated from high school. Ginsberg, in her biography, says she hung a large picture of her mother in her office where she was serving as the

Justice of the U.S. Supreme Court. Every day before leaving office, she would spend some moments looking at her picture and thinking, *My mother would have been proud of me.*

Jane Goodall

This is a story of a girl who was given a stuffed chimpanzee, and she developed a deep love for them. She probably never dreamed that she would reach where she did without a college degree. She achieved great things and surprised the world with her outstanding research on chimpanzees. It would seem that love for animals, especially chimpanzees, was in her blood.

Valerie Jane Morris-Goodall, an English primatologist and anthropologist, is considered the world's foremost expert on chimpanzees. She is best known for her 60-year study of social and family interactions of wild chimpanzees since she first went to Gombe Stream National Park in Tanzania in 1960.

Jane, as she is best known, was born on April 3, 1934, in London in the United Kingdom. Her father Mortimer Herbert Morris-Goodall was a telephone engineer who later became a racing car driver for Aston-Martin. Her mother Vann Morris-Goodall started as a secretary and later became a novelist. Jane grew up in a middle-class English family.

She grew up in a loving family and was a happy child who liked the outdoors and loved playing in the neighborhood. She wanted to explore things. When she was one year old, her father gave her a toy, a stuffed chimpanzee. She was thrilled. In 2017, she told CNN "When I was 10, I dreamt of going to Africa, living with animals and writing books about them."

Jane attended elementary schools in Bournemouth, her hometown, about 170 miles from London and developed a fondness for reading. At the age of 11, she began high school at Uplands private school for girls. A year later, she formed a nature club called the Alligator Club.

It is surprising how this young girl was infatuated by the animal world and wildlife. No other member in the family had either worked in wildlife, nor did they have an interest. Sharing her childhood with CNN, she talked about her dream of staying in Africa with animals and writing about them. "Everybody laughed at me as I was just a little girl, and we didn't have money and World War II was raging." It is an astonishing and most unusual thought of a 10-year-old girl.

Graduating from high school, Jane could not go to college as it was expensive, and her parents could not afford college fees. She therefore wanted to pursue her interest in writing. But her mother persuaded her to first have a "solid degree in hand" that could make her financially independent. This encouragement by mothers, of a practical approach to their daughter's lives, is a theme in many of the celebrities' histories. Successful women often credit to their mothers for inspiring them to get a good education, pursue a career, and be financially independent.

Justice Ginsberg's mother instilled in her the ambition for attending the best schools and excelling in her education so she could stand on her own feet. Ginsberg's mother painstakingly saved for her education, but she was always on full scholarships. Even the life of the current Vice-President Kamala Harris depicts the same.

Jane's mother's advice was a sound one as in those days secretaries and typists were much in demand. And, as long as businesses and offices existed, secretaries would be needed. Jane's mother advised her to get a qualification that would guarantee her a job.

Jane enrolled at London's Queens Secretarial College, graduated the next year, and worked at Oxford University and in a London filmmaking company. She found office work boring. When a friend invited her to Kenya, Africa, to visit her, she jumped at the offer. Exploring the jungles of Africa was her long cherished dream, and she had read widely about African wildlife and forests which she so fervently wished to visit.

To raise funds for her travel to Kenya, Jane returned to her hometown Bournemouth working as a waitress. She reached Kenya in 1957 by boat and was fascinated by the wildlife. She explored the Nairobi farm with her friend. She had read about the famous paleoanthropologist Dr. Louis S.B. Leakey at the museum of natural history. She made an appointment to see him. According to Anita Silvey, author of a book on Goodall, Leaky was looking for someone who was "observant and not blinded by scientific theory." Wanting to test Jane, he took her around the forests in his Jeep and was amazed that Jane was able to name all the animals in the area.

Leakey was impressed by Jane's lack of scientific training and no formal academic background or degree in wildlife. Yet, she knew a great deal about Africa and its wildlife and was a true observer. Leakey hired Jane as his assistant.

He tested her observational skills, giving her two sets of playing cards, both upside down, and asked Jane which one was red out of the two—red and blue packs. Jane pointed to one, which was correct. She later explained that she guessed that the one pack that had all corners bent had to be different.

Leakey wanted Jane to work observing the social lives of chimpanzees at the forest of Gombe in Tanzania. Jane was thrilled and being in Africa was a turning point in her life. She never dreamed she'd be working under such a renowned person as Dr. Leakey. This is what we call "destiny." Jane could not have imagined that she could go to Africa, live with chimpanzees, observe them closely, and play with them.

Leakey raised funds for Jane's work initially. He deserves credit for Jane's outstanding research and later pressurizing *National Geographic* to release more funds for further research that made Jane famous. Jane's major discoveries about chimpanzees were that they made tools like humans, were not vegetarian, and they had a hierarchy in their social life just as humans did.

Jane had to overcome many obstacles in the African jungle. There were dangers of serious diseases, such as malaria, smallpox, cholera and yellow fever; weather of dusty storms, gusty winds; and poisonous species of snakes, scorpions, wild spiders and wasps, etc. Living in the dark, dense forest surrounded by all these was a challenge. In one of the references, it is stated that at night the sound of the wild buffalos running, poisonous cobras hanging on trees and rivers flooded with crocodiles were the most frightful scenes. But Jane and her mother (her mother accompanied Jane in the forest for some time), fearlessly faced them all, and she pursued her mission. At some point, both suffered from malaria but soon recovered.

In 1963, *National Geographic* printed a special issue of Jane's work accompanied by photographs by Hugo van Lawick. Her article, "My Life with Wild Chimpanzees," was instrumental in creating awareness about her work. It was a historic moment and an achievement for Jane, Leakey, and Hugo. Jane traveled to lecture and talk about her findings and her life with the chimpanzees. Later, Hugo and Jane married and had a son.

Despite her success, Jane faced discrimination from the scientific world of paleoanthropologists and anthropologists who were not convinced about Jane's research. They labeled her as "naïve," without any scientific training or professional degrees, and said her research was based on "unorthodox practices."

Jane delivered two memorable lectures. One was to the Zoological Society of London's primate symposium in 1962 and the other at Washington D.C. in 1964, her first public lecture in the United States. After the first lecture, she was criticized by scientists despite the fact that the crowd was impressed and so was the famous zoologist and author Desmond Morris.

Her public lecture in the United States created a revolution, and she became famous after that. The committee of *National Geographic* editors were skeptical about her performance, the content of the lecture, and her ability to deliver it. But the lecture was "majestically inspiring and mesmerizing." Even Jane herself termed it as one "beyond her farthest dreams."

Jane's pathbreaking research on chimpanzees in the Gombe forest of Africa brought her fame. If Jane had a Ph.D. before her observations at Gombe, she probably would have been nominated for a Nobel Prize. In 1966, she got a Ph.D. from Cambridge University, without an undergraduate degree. Leakey made this possible and remarked, "She was one of the few ever to be admitted without a college degree."

With Hugo, Jane wrote several books and founded famous research institutes, such as Gombe Research Institute and established a philanthropic program, Shoots and Roots, aimed at engaging young people with conservation and preservation of wildlife. She served on the board of the Nonhuman Rights Project and was named a UN Messenger of Peace, an award of highest honor of the United Nations given by then Secretary General-Kofi Annan in 2004. She also taught at Stanford University that enabled her to set up an "outdoor permit facility."

After 10 years of marriage, Jane and Hugo divorced. Later, she married a Tanzanian government official who passed away after five years. Today, Jane lives in her home in London. She was touring 300 days a year, lecturing at various places in the world, but had to take a break due to the Covid pandemic.

Jane's life is admirable as she achieved much success with no college education in the beginning. She pursued her dreams with determination and devotion while facing discrimination. She has left a legacy, a powerful image and an extraordinary lesson to the world that will be remembered for a long time.

Ruth Bader Ginsberg
Ruth Bader Ginsberg was a renowned Supreme Court Justice, and an example of courage, determination, perseverance, and fearlessness. Through her life, we can see how values shape our lives, which is the underlying theme of this book. There is an abundance of literature that suggests that Ruth, like her mother, also aimed high. "*Nothing but the absolute best*" was the motto of her life.

Ruth Bader Ginsberg was born in New York in 1933 in Brooklyn, New York. A daughter of immigrant parents and grandparents, her mother,

Celia, was a born in America to parents who migrated from Poland and her father, Nathan, was from Ukraine, which was then part of Russia. Those were Depression days, and scarcity was on the horizon. Ruth's parents, both employed in factories, worked hard.

Her mother Celia was more authoritarian and a disciplinarian than the father. She was a smart woman with foresight, ambitious, and very goal oriented. Her motto in life was to achieve the best by living a life of truth, modesty, and righteousness, being economically independent and earning enough to ensure a comfortable future. She wanted Ruth to receive quality education in the finest institutions of higher learning, win laurels, and be successful. Towards this, Ruth's mother worked hard and saved money to send the children to the best schools. Living during the Depression, she was familiar with the life of scarcity, poverty, and an uncertain future. Ruth imbibed these values and worked hard, being at the top of her class and getting admission to the best schools. She was driven by her mother's aspirations to be the star and did indeed become one.

With a Jewish up bringing, both parents were firm believers of the virtues of modesty, truthfulness, celibacy, controlling anger, righteousness, and achieving the highest ladder of success in life. It is not easy to follow these ideals, but Ruth did, and for this gave credit to her mother. At every milestone of success, she would say, "My mother would have been proud of me."

Ruth's life was full of challenges. The first was managing high school and her mother's illness. For four years, she watched her mother gradually dying. The day before graduation, Ruth's mother died. How painful it would have been for Ruth, mourning her mother's departure, while her teachers brought home her medals. However, for Ruth, these painful moments were like energetic shots of inspiration, like shooting stars in which her mother's memories were buried. They guided her like a torch to move on to accomplish her goals that her mother very much wanted. The death of her mother was a profound loss. She grew up *"with the smell of death,"* she later said.

Ruth was awarded a full scholarship to Cornell University, a dream cherished by her mother, and then went on to Columbia Law School. She struggled and sacrificed to achieve what she did, just as her mother did— saving for Ruth's education, working in garment factories, traveling in subways, taking care of the home and family, struggling with cervical cancer, and succumbing to it on a day before Ruth's graduation.

Ruth met Martin (Marty) Ginsberg at Cornell on a blind date. According to Biography.com, "Marty, already a sophomore, had urged a friend to set him up with the cute new freshman. Before long he realized that this petite beauty was a cerebral powerhouse, an observation that wasn't lost on his soon-to-be inseparable companion." Through all her years at Cornell, male students, including the Dean, remarked that she had taken a man's place. Ruth, however, excelled and stood first in her class.

The two married in June 1954 after Ruth graduated from Cornell.

After Martin finished his first year at Harvard Law School, he was drafted to the U.S. Army. Ruth accompanied Martin to Sill, Oklahoma, taking a break from her studies. She was pregnant with their first child. At Sill, Ruth accepted a lower pay and rank while working at a job that was higher ranked. In Oklahoma, the Ginsbergs began adjusting to their strengths and weaknesses as a couple. For example, Ruth knew she was not a good cook. Marty decided to take over. As Marty said, "I was frightened by the thought of a lifetime of reheated tuna casseroles." He developed a reputation as a "culinary wunderkind." Ruth later recalled, "He was the first boy I met who knew I had a brain."

After two years in Oklahoma, both continued their studies at Harvard Law School. In Marty's senior year, he was diagnosed with testicular cancer. Ruth had to manage a three-year-old daughter, the house, her studies, and Marty's sickness. She requested his classmates to take notes in duplicate with carbon paper, which she typed up at night for Marty, who graduated *magna cum laude*, although missing classes the whole semester.

Marty joined a renowned tax law firm at New York and became one of the leading tax attorneys. Ruth was still in her final year at Harvard. She transferred to Columbia Law School to be closer in distance to Marty, although it might have been harder on her as she had to adjust to her new environment and that, too, in her final year of graduate work. Ruth rose to this challenge by getting a first in class in Columbia. She was also the first woman to serve on the board of editors of *Columbia Law Review*.

Ginsberg's achievements were no protection against discrimination. In 2016, speaking to CBS on not getting any job offers despite graduating first in her class at Columbia, she said, "I had three strikes against me. One I was Jewish, two I was a woman, but the killer was that I was the mother of a four-year-old child." This situation, like many times before, proved to be "boosters" for Ruth. Instead of feeling inferior, sad, and frustrated, Ruth took it as a challenge and was more determined to fight inequality.

Ruth became a powerhouse and an authority on discriminatory laws. She won many cases. The court marveled at the petite woman of small stature, standing boldly in front of the Supreme Court and judges and contesting cases with such a forceful and flawless voice and convincing arguments that stunned both audience and jury alike. In 1993, President Bill Clinton appointed Ruth to the U.S. Supreme Court. She held this position for just over 27 years until her death.

Of all the important rulings, the three that stand out are the Affordable Care Act or Obamacare, Same Sex Marriage, and Equality of all for Admission to the Schools of Army, Navy and Defense. The Affordable Care Act gave power to the federal government to continue providing subsidies to Americans who purchase health care through state or federally operated institutions. She sided with the other judges on this important legislation that turned into a majority. She was instrumental in making same sex marriage legal for all states.

Ruth's challenges continued. In 2010, Martin passed away from cancer. Ruth was shocked and said that for the first time in her life she felt "alone" and lonely. After 56 years of marriage, they were like two sides of the same coin, supporting, and helping each other. Ruth herself fought a 20-year battle against different cancers—of the colon, pancreas, lung, and liver. But she continued working till the end.

In a 2015 interview with MSNBC, Ginsberg remarked, "I want to be remembered as someone who used whatever talent she had to do her work to the best of her ability. And to repair tears in her society, to make things a little better by whatever ability she has. To do something, as my colleague David Souter would say, 'outside myself'. Cause I've gotten much more satisfaction for the things that I've done for which I was not paid."

When Ruth died in September 2020, the BBC posted:

US Supreme Court Justice Ruth Bader Ginsburg, the history-making jurist, feminist icon and national treasure, has died, aged 87.

Ruth was outspoken during President Donald Trump's Presidency. She was furious at his lack of respect for the judiciary and other institutions. National Public Radio (NPR) reported that Ginsburg's final statement as dictated to her granddaughter Clara from her death bed was, "My most fervent wish is that I will not be replaced until a new President is installed."

Ruth Ginsberg will be remembered as a person who made history despite being an immigrant and coming from humble beginnings. She is an example of fearlessness, courage, perseverance, dedication, and justice. Her eye-opening handling of cases of inequality point to the depth of discriminatory practices prevalent in society.

In Ruth's life three personalities, besides her mother, inspired her. Her husband Martin and two professors at Cornell. Martin was the inspiration at every stage of her life. He campaigned for her when she was nominated for the Supreme Court and encouraged her in everything she did. His support was like a radar in the storm. At Cornell, writer Vladimir Nabokov inspired her writing skills, and Robert Cushman, known for his mastery of constitution law, inspired Ruth to aspire for a career in law.

Ruth never forgot where she came from. In March 2021, Charles Kaiser wrote in *The Guardian*, "Two and a half years ago, at a naturalization ceremony for newly minted Americans, Ruth Bader Ginsburg was asked: "What is the difference between a bookkeeper in New York City's garment district and a supreme court justice?" Her answer: "One generation … the difference between opportunities available to my mother and those afforded to me."

Thank you, Justice Ginsberg, for your contributions. From your life, it is clear that the *Values* you imbibed from your parents, teachers and life partner influenced you greatly, and we all benefitted from them.

And finally, in 2021, in the U.S. election Kamala Harris, became vice-president. A daughter of immigrants, immensely inspired by her mother to be "someone that the world can be proud of," set high goals and achieved them. She became the first woman to be elected as the vice president, the first Afro-American, and the first Asian. Her biography and life have many parallels to the lives of Goodall and Ginsberg.

Part Three
Anecdotes and Quotes

Introduction to Part Three

Parts I and II feature the personal stories in which *values* had a profound impact on the lives of the writers. In this section of the book, I try to leave the readers with unique quotes written by well-known persons on the themes in Parts I and II. The quotes are on perseverance, faith, fear, hope, hard work, service, equality, success, and charity.

There are quotes, sayings, and mini stories from text messages, emails, and YouTube videos sent to me. Therefore, there is no authorship as such. When I know the source, I mention it. There are some anecdotes, which I enjoyed reading and wanted to share in this section.

For me, this is a beautiful way to end the book. This section reconfirms, redefines, reemphasizes, and recaps the worth of everlasting *values* that inspire us and leave a mark on us.

FEAR OF DEATH

A sick man turned to his doctor as he was preparing to leave the examination room and said, "Doctor, I am afraid to die. Tell me what lies on the other side."

Very quietly, the doctor said, "I don't know." The doctor was holding the handle of the door; on the other side came a sound of scratching and whining, and as he opened the door, a dog sprang into the room and leaped on him with excitement.

Turning to the patient, the doctor said, "Did you notice my dog? He has never been in this room before. He did not know what was inside. He knew nothing except that his master was here, and when the door opened, he sprang in without fear. I know little of what is on the other side of death, but I do know one thing. I know my Master is there and that is enough."

Lesson: It takes faith to overcome fear. Salutations to all Divine Masters
Received as a text message to me.

WHEN GRATITUDE BRINGS HAPPINESS

A famous writer was in his study. He picked up his pen and started writing:

Last year, I had a surgery, and my gall bladder was removed. I had to stay stuck to the bed due to this surgery for a long time.

The same year I reached the age of 60 years and had to give up my favorite job. I had spent 30 years of my life in this publishing company.

The same year I experienced the sorrow of the death of my father.

And in the same year my son failed in his medical exam because he had a car accident. He had to stay in bed at the hospital with the cast on for several days.

The destruction of my car was another loss.

At the end he wrote: *Oh God! It was such a bad year!!*

When the writer's wife entered the room, she found her husband looking sad and lost in his thoughts. From behind his back, she read what was written on the paper. She left the room silently and came back with another piece of paper and placed it on side of her husband's writing.

When the writer saw this paper, he found his name written on it with following lines:

Last year I finally got rid of my gall bladder due to which I had spent years in pain. I turned 60 with sound health and retired from my job. Now I can utilize my time to write something better with more focus and peace.

The same year my father, at the age of 95, without depending on anyone or without any critical condition, met his Creator.

The same year, God blessed my son with a new life. My car was destroyed but my son stayed alive without a disability.

At the end she wrote: *This year was an immense blessing of God and it passed well!!!*

The writer was happy and amazed at such beautiful and encouraging interpretation of the happenings in his life in that year.

Lesson: *"Always look at the brighter side of any event in life."*

GOD'S WIFE

Author and lecturer Leo Buscaglia talked about a contest he was asked to judge. The purpose of the contest was to find the most caring child. There were five winners. Each story of the winners is a lesson by itself. The last story, "God's Wife," was the most powerful. Below it was the remark: "it will knock your socks off." This story is part of a collection of stories compiled by Ivan Raley in the *Collection of Stories* by Sunbury Press. https://seniorchatters.co.uk/gods-wife-by-leo-buscaglia/

An eyewitness account from New York City, on a cold day in December, some years ago: A little boy, about 10-years-old, was standing before a shoe store on the roadway, barefooted, peering through the window, and shivering with cold.

A lady approached the young boy and said, "My, but you're in such deep thought staring in that window!"

"I was asking God to give me a pair of shoes," was the boy's reply.

The lady took him by the hand, went into the store, and asked the clerk to get half a dozen pairs of socks for the boy. She then asked if he could give her a basin of water and a towel. He quickly brought them to her.

She took the little fellow to the back of the store and, removing her gloves, knelt down, washed his little feet, and dried them with the towel. By this time, the clerk had returned with the socks. Placing a pair upon the boy's feet, she purchased him a pair of shoes. She tied up the remaining pairs of socks and gave them to him. She patted him on the head and said, "No doubt, you will be more comfortable now."

As she turned to go, the astonished kid caught her by the hand and, looking up into her face with tears in his eyes, asked her: "Are you God's wife?"

Lesson: In a child's heart and mind there is a belief that all things pure, noble, and truthful reside in GOD, who is the Savior, and will bring you relief when you are helpless. God is generally but not always, personified as a man, and in this incident, when the child encounters a person showing love and kindness, who happens to be a woman, he could only define and place her as God's Wife. Interesting.

REWARDING GOOD KARMA (DEEDS)

An Indian woman would make one extra roti or a tortilla like bread of whole wheat flour when cooking her meals. She kept it on the kitchen windowsill, facing the road, saying a hungry or needy person might take it. Every day after a few hours that roti disappeared. One day she saw a Pandit (priest) from the nearest temple picking up the roti. He said "My dear child, I only eat meals that are given to me with love from my well-wishers. This is a donation and blessings of my people. If someday I do not get enough food, I go hungry and accept whatever there is."

The Pandit then told the woman, "Remember your bad karma will go away and one day, the fruits of your good action like this will come back to you."

The woman thought about this, searched her soul and said to herself, "I do not think I have knowingly committed any act that would be bad karma. So why is this Pandit saying this to me?"

The routine continued and every day the Pandit recited his sermon. One day she noticed that the roti lay on the windowsill, dry and crumbled. She got worried that the Pandit must be sick. One day, the doorbell rang. Opening her front door, she was amazed to see her son who was overseas, standing there, pale and hungry, he had lost a lot of weight. She embraced him and was emotional.

He said, "Ma, I have not eaten for two days, and the country was infested with cholera (those days it was a scary disease similar to the Coronavirus), so I was praying to reach home safe and healthy. In his hand he had the crumbled roti she had made that day, which he had been eating. "A Panditji asked me why I look so pale. I said I am really hungry; he gave me the roti."

The mother now understood the meaning of the Pandit's sermon. She told her son about the roti and the Pandit. The son ran to the temple and brought the Pandit with him saying, "Today, we will eat my mother's cooking to our hearts content. Come let us eat together."

Lesson: Never give up doing noble things that give you pleasure and helping people, even if you are frustrated and think no one cares. One day, your bad karma will be washed, and good karma will be rewarded.

Received from YouTube

GOD'S BOXES
I have in my hands two boxes,
Which God gave me to hold.
He said, "Put all your sorrows in the black box,
And all your joys in the gold."
I heeded His words, and in the two boxes,
Both my joys and sorrows I stored,
But though the gold became heavier each day,
The black was as light as before.
With curiosity, I opened the black,
I wanted to find out why,
And I saw, in the base of the box, a hole,
Which my sorrows had fallen out by.
I showed the hole to God, and mused,
"I wonder where my sorrows could be!"
He smiled a gentle smile and said,
"My child, they're all here with me."
I asked God why He gave me the boxes,
Why the gold and the black with the hole?
"My child, the gold is for you to count your blessings,
The black is for you to let go."
We should consider all of our friends a blessing.
Send this to a friend today just to let them know you
Are thinking of them and that they are a joy in your life.
A ball is a circle, no beginning, no end.
It keeps us together like our Circle of Friends.
But the treasure inside for you to see,
Is the treasure of friendship you've granted to me.

Lesson: Count your blessings. Let go the unpleasant deeds of others.
Email from a friend on Christmas Day.

ON PATIENCE
Patience is wonderful medicine. The one who has learned it and practices it, has reached heavenly peace.

By Guru Nanak, founder of Sikhism—a religion originated in India. He was the first of the 10 Sikh gurus.

I'VE LEARNED
- I've learned … That the best classroom in the world is at the feet of an elderly person.
- I've learned … That when you're in love, it shows.
- I've learned … That just one person saying to me, "You've made my day!" MAKES MY DAY.
- I've learned … That having a child fall asleep in your arms is one of the most peaceful feelings in the world.
- I've learned … That being kind is more important than being right.
- I've learned … That you should never say no to a gift from a child.
- I've learned … That I can always pray for someone when I don't have the strength to help him in some other way.
- I've learned … That no matter how serious your life requires you to be, everyone needs a friend to act goofy with.
- I've learned … That sometimes all a person needs is a hand to hold and a heart to understand.
- I've learned … That simple walks with my father around the block on summer nights when I was a child did wonders for me as an adult.
- I've learned … That life is like a roll of toilet paper. The closer it gets to the end, the faster it goes.
- I've learned … That we should be glad God doesn't give us everything we ask for.
- I've learned … That money doesn't buy class or command respect.
- I've learned … That it's those small daily happenings that make life so spectacular.
- I've learned … That under everyone's hard shell is someone who wants to be appreciated, respected, and loved.
- I've learned … That to ignore the facts does not change the facts.
- I've learned … That love alone and surpassing time, heals all wounds.

- I've learned … That no one is perfect until you fall in love with them.
- I've learned … That life is tough, but a human is tougher.
- I've learned … That opportunities are never lost; someone will take the ones you miss.
- I've learned … That when you harbor bitterness, happiness will dock elsewhere.
- I've learned … That I wish I could have told my mom that I love her one more time before she passed away.
- I've learned … That one should keep his words both soft and tender, because tomorrow he may have to eat them.
- I've learned … That a smile is an inexpensive way to improve your looks., understand it and genuinely PRACTICE it silently!
- I've learned … That when your newly born grandchild holds your little finger in his little fist, that you're hooked for life.
- I've learned … That everyone wants to live on top of the mountain, but all the happiness and growth occurs while you're climbing than once there, you simply have to practice to ENJOY it.

By Andy Rooney, American radio and television writer best known for his weekly broadcast "A Few Minutes with Andy Rooney," a part of the CBS News program 60 Minutes from 1978 to 2011.

GO SLOW LIFE
Ahistay chal Zindagi,
Abhi kai Karz Chukana baaki hai.
Kuch Dard Mitana baaki hai,
Kuch Farz Nibhana baaki hai.
Raftaar mein Tere chalne se,
Kuchh Rooth gaye, Kuch Chhut gaye.
Roothon ko Manana baaki hai,
Roothon ko Hasana baaki hai.
Kuch Hasraatein abhi Adhuri hain,
Kuch Kaam bhi aur Zaruri hai.
Khwahishen jo Ghut Gayi is Dil mein,
Unko Dafnana baaki hai.
Kuch Rishte Ban kar Toot gaye,
Kuch Judte-Judte Chhut gaye.
Un Tootte-Chhutte Rishton ke
Zakhmon ko Mitana baki hai.
Tu Aage chal Main aata hoon,
Kya chhod Tujhe Ji paunga?
In Saanson par Haqq hai Jinka,
Unko Samjhaana baaki hai.
Aahista chal Zindagi,
Abhi kai Karz Chukana baaki hai .
(Received on my iPhone)

Translation in English by Manjulika Koshal
Oh, life go slow, some debts have to be paid.
Some duties have to be done; some sorrows have to be mitigated.
In your speed, some are left behind, some are forgotten.
Have yet to cheer up the ones annoyed,
Have to amend past mistakes with the annoyed.
Some relationships broke after being made, and
Some got broken when they were on the verge of being made.
The broken relationships have to be healed,
Those who have the right on these breaths, need to be made understandable.
Go slow oh life some debts still have to be paid.

By Gulzar, the well-known Indian lyricist, poet, author, screenwriter, and film director. His original name is Sampooran Singh Kalra, and he was born in 1934.

ON FRIENDSHIP AND OLD FRIENDS
Slowly, slowly we age,
And life becomes a book of memories.
Sometimes one really misses someone,
And sometimes life is spent with these memories.
The treasures of the ocean, do not come on its banks,
So, in life old friends do not come back.
Live oh my friend, these moments with smiles,
Because the era of friendship will not come back.

By Dilip Kumar or Mohammed Yusuf Khan, born 1922, an Indian actor and philanthropist. (original in Hindi and translated by Manjulika Koshal).

A LESSON IN SELF APPRAISAL
A little boy walked into the pharmacy to use the phone.
"Can you give me the job of cutting your lawn?" said the boy into the phone.
"I already have someone cutting the lawn," said the lady on the other end of the phone.
"I will cut your lawn for half the price for what the other person is doing now," the boy said.
"I am very satisfied with the other person who is doing the job," the lady said.
"But I will even cut the edges and sweep the curbs and sidewalks," the boy said. "You will have the prettiest lawn in the town."
"No, thank you", the lady replied.
Smiling, the boy hung up. The storekeeper who listened to the entire conversation, approached the boy.
"I like your positive attitude and spirit," said the storeowner. "Would you like a job here in my store?"
"No, thank you," said the boy.
"But you were just pleading for one," the shopkeeper said.
"No Sir, I was just checking my performance level. I am the one who is cutting the lawn of the lady I was talking to."

Lesson: This is "self-appraisal." Every time you evaluate others, evaluate yourself. Only then we can grow as people.
(Received on WhatsApp)

A JOURNEY CALLED LIFE

A mouse looked through the crack in the wall to see the farmer and his wife open a package.

What food might this contain? the mouse wondered. He was devastated to discover it was a mousetrap.

Retreating to the farmyard, the mouse proclaimed this warning: "There is a mousetrap in the house! There is a mousetrap in the house!"

The chicken clucked and scratched, raised her head and said, "Mr. Mouse, I can tell this is a grave concern to you, but it is of no consequence to me. I cannot be bothered by it."

The mouse turned to the pig and told him, "There is a mousetrap in the house. There is a mousetrap in the house!"

The pig sympathized, but said, "I am so very sorry, Mr. Mouse, but there is nothing I can do about it."

The mouse turned to the cow and said, "There is a mousetrap in the house! There is a mousetrap in the house!"

The cow said, "Wow, Mr. Mouse. I'm sorry for you, but it's no skin off my nose."

So, the mouse returned to the house, head down and dejected, to face the farmer's mousetrap… Alone…

That very night a sound was heard throughout the house—the sound of a mousetrap, catching its prey. The farmer's wife rushed to see what was caught. In the darkness, she did not see it. It was a venomous snake whose tail was caught in the trap. The snake bit the farmer's wife. The farmer rushed her to the hospital.

When she returned home, she still had a fever. Everyone knows you treat a fever with fresh chicken soup. So, the farmer took his hatchet to the farmyard for the soup's main ingredient. But his wife's sickness continued. Friends and neighbors came to sit with her around the clock. To feed them, the farmer butchered the pig. But, alas, the farmer's wife did not get well. She died.

Many people came for her funeral, so the farmer had the cow slaughtered to provide enough meat for all of them for the funeral luncheon. And the mouse looked upon it all from his crack in the wall with great sadness.

So, the next time you hear someone is facing a problem and you think it doesn't concern you, remember when one of us is threatened, we are all at risk. We are all involved in this journey called life.

Lesson: We must watch out for one another and encourage one another.

Excerpted from This Journey called Life *by Christina Burns, a compilation of poems that seek to make sense of the obstacles that we encounter in life, the questions we have, the people we encounter and the overall experiences we have in life.*

WHERE IS HOPE HIDING OUT TODAY?
Life often feels like one big transition.
We are on the road, between chapters,
Losing one thing and finding another,
Taking a leap, taking a chance, flying,
Falling, getting up, waking up, doing
Our best—so why expect the worst?
Why not hope? Why not look closely
Enough to see the bright side …
In the world, in you, in every moment?

From On the Bright Side — Finding Hope in Every Today, *by Jim Howard, illustrated by Daniel Miyares. Hallmark Licensing Inc, 2010.* Published by *"Sunbury Press, 2016"*

WHO HURTS YOU?

When Abraham Lincoln became the President of the United States, his father was a shoemaker. Some people were offended that a shoemaker's son should become the president. On the first day, as Lincoln entered to give his inaugural address, in the middle of his talk one man stood up. He was rich aristocrat. He said, "Mr. Lincoln, you should not forget that your father used to make shoes for my family."

The whole Senate laughed.

Lincoln looked at the man directly in his eyes and said, "Sir, I know that my father used to make shoes for your family and there will be many others in this crowd for whom he made the shoes because he made shoes the way nobody else can. He was a creator. His shoes were not just shoes: he poured his whole soul into them.

"I want to ask you, 'have you any complaints?' because I know how to make shoes myself. If you have any complaints, I can make you another pair of shoes. But as far as I know, nobody has ever complained about my father's shoes. He was a genius; a great creator and I am proud of my father."

The Senate members couldn't understand what kind of man Abraham Lincoln was. He was proud because his father did a good job so well, with so much enthusiasm, such a passion and perfection.

Lesson: It does not matter what you do, what matters is *how* you do it of your own accord, with your own vision, with your own love. Then whatever you touch becomes gold. *Received on WhatsApp.*

ON SUCCESS
"Always bear in mind that your own resolution to succeed is more important than any other thing." *Abraham Lincoln*

"Success is getting what you want. Happiness is wanting what you get." *B. R. Hayden.*

"Success is a journey, not a destination." *Ben Sweetland.*

"The secret of success in life is for a man to be ready for his opportunity when it comes." *Benjamin Disraeli.*

"I don't know the key to success, but the key to failure is trying to please everybody." *Bill Cosby.*

"The secret of success is to be in harmony with existence, to be always calm, to let each wave of life wash us a little farther up the shore." *Cyril Connolly.*

"All of us are born for a reason, but all of us don't discover why. Success in life has nothing to do with what you gain in life or accomplish for yourself. It's what you do for others." *Danny Thomas.*

"Don't confuse fame with success. Madonna is one; Helen Keller is the other." *Erma Bombeck.*

"Success is not the result of spontaneous combustion. You must first set yourself on fire." *Fred Shero.*

"Success does not consist in never making mistakes but in never making the same one a second time." *George Bernard Shaw.*

"A strong, positive self-image is the best possible preparation for success." *Joyce Brothers.*

"Failure is success if we learn from it." *Malcolm S. Forbes.*

"The first step toward success is taken when you refuse to be a captive of the environment in which you first find yourself." *Mark Caine.*

"True success is overcoming the fear of being unsuccessful."
Paul Sweeney.

"Get up one time more than you're knocked down."
Peter's Principle of Success.

"Most people who succeed in the face of seemingly impossible conditions are people who simply don't know how to quit."
Robert Schuller.

"The truth is that all of us attain the greatest success and happiness possible in this life whenever we use our native capacities to their greatest extent." *Smiley Blanton.*

"When your physical environment is in alignment with your aspiration, success becomes the norm." *Susan St Lawrence.*

"The most important single ingredient in the formula of success is knowing how to get along with people." *Theodore Roosevelt.*

"The way to succeed is to double your error rate." *Thomas Watson.*

"Dictionary is the only place that success comes before work. Hard work is the price we must pay for success. I think you can accomplish anything if you're willing to pay the price." *Vince Lombardi.*

"Success is the ability to go from failure to failure without losing your enthusiasm." *Winston Churchill.*

"Success is the maximum utilization of the ability that you have."
Zig Ziglar.

I have collected the above quotes over a period of 30 years from various magazines, books, letters, my parents and family discussions.

WHAT GOOD IS...

What good is a beautiful face if it lacks radiance?

What good is a smile if it is superficial?

What good is a healthy heart if it has no love?

What good is friendship if it lacks sincerity?

What good is a devoted wife if she lacks compassion?

What good is a beautiful piece of art if no one can understand the artist's intent?

What good is a couple deeply in love, if there is no spirit of sacrifice for one another?

What good is Mother's Day if it does not evoke cherished memories of your mother?

What good is a palatial house if the feeling of home is absent?

What good is a large bank balance if it is not spent on the less fortunate?

What good is a flower if it has no fragrance?

What good is a human life if it has not been lived to the fullest?

What good is a humming bee if it only stings?

What good is a tall, elegant tree, if it cannot provide shade to a tired visitor?

What good is an avid researcher if his life consists of only research?

What good is a husband if he is only a breadwinner?

AN ANECDOTE FROM A FRIEND

I had a very emotional encounter last year and decided to write it down on the pages of my Mémoire immortelle. Allow me to share the same with you all.

Last week, my husband and I decided to visit one of my dad-in-law's old friends living in Delhi. He is a retired officer from the Indian Army. They are an exceptionally fine couple, well spoken, very well read, and widely travelled. They had a son who they lost during the Kargil War. However, they never show any trace of pain on their face. It would seem all is well but for the deep-set wrinkles on the mother's face, which tell a different tale altogether. Uncle's countless jokes and humorous conversation do a brilliant job of camouflaging their pain.

We had a wonderful time with them. Since they are old associates of my dad-in-law (he is from Indian army, too), my husband had a gala time revisiting old memory of his school days. Uncle and Aunty told funny stories, and I kept laughing like a fearless kid. Soon their caretaker served us a well-organized tea, and with each simmering sip came even more interesting chain of events from uncle's well-preserved memory bank.

I was wondering as to how could they talk endlessly without a pause. I realized why. After we were done with tea, I got up to collect all the cups and the other things to keep in a tray so that I could keep those back in the kitchen. But I was stopped by a very authoritative and strong voice: "No, please do not move those cups from there."

I was taken aback and looked at Aunty if I had ruffled his feathers by any action of mine. But then, Aunty looked at uncle and said softly, "Tusi bhi na….bacche nu dara ditta…thora aram naal bhi keh sakde ho." ("You really, you are frightening the child. You could have said it a little gently.")

Uncle then sat next to me, held my hand, and put the other hand on my head. He said, "Beta ji, in cups ko aise hee rehne do…subah tak nahi uthayenge…kuch toh ehsaas hoga ki zindagi yahan ayi thi." ("Child, leave the cups, we'll pick it up in the morning. Let us feel that today life came to visit us.")

He said the house always remained clean as nothing is moved or disturbed. So, let the cups stay that way; we will cherish the sight of it. And promise me that you will visit again with your sons. I hugged him and assured him that I would be back with my sons.

I, too, like my house to be meticulously organized and make sure my boys follow suit. But unfortunately, my younger one still believes in living like a caveman. So, when I was lecturing him today after seeing the condition of his room, I reminded of this episode and suddenly, I stopped, and gave him a suffocating hug, leaving him confused to the core.

I think that making time to visit our parents, relatives or old friends does not cost us much.

न मिट सकेंगी ये तन्हाईयाँ मगर ऐ दोस (*Dost*)
जो तू भी हो तो तबियत ज़रा बहल जाए.

"Na mit skegi yeh tanhaee aye mere dost pur agar tu bhi toh saath hote toh tabiat bahal jaatee."

The meaning of above saying is, *"This sadness would be with me, but if you were here my friend, the mood would have perked up."*
Source Unknown

Note: The Kargil War was between India and Pakistan in 1999. The Kargil war was fought on territorial issues and was resolved when India re-captured its side of the Line of Control.

QUOTES
Old friends are like Gold
New friends are Diamonds,
If you get Diamonds, do not throw away the Gold,
Because only Gold can mount the Diamonds.
A.P.J Abdul Kalam, President of India from 2002-2005.

"I will not say I failed 1,000 times; I will say that I discovered 1,000 ways that can cause failure." *Thomas Alva Edison.*

"If someone feels that they have never made a mistake in their life, then it means they had never tried a new thing in their life." *Albert Einstein.*

"Believing everybody is dangerous but believing nobody is more dangerous." *Abraham Lincoln.*

"Never break four things in life: Trust, Relations, Promise and Heart because when they break, they do not make noise, but it pains a lot." *Charles Dickens.*

"If you judge people you have no time to love them. If we cannot love the person whom we see, how can we love God whom we cannot see?" *Mother Teresa.*

"Three sentences for getting Success. Know more than others. Work more than others. Expect less than others." *William Shakespeare.*

Be a good person but do not waste time to prove it.
You are the driver of your own life, do not let anyone steal your seat.
If you want to be happy, do not dwell in the past, do not worry about the future, focus fully in the present.
Weak people seek revenge, Strong people forgive, Intelligent people ignore.
The less you respond to negative people, the more peaceful your life will become.
Be the same person, privately, publicly, and personally.
Do not teach your children to be rich. Educate them to be happy, so that when they grow up, they will know the *value* of things, not just the *price*.

Gautam Buddha, spiritual leader and founder of Buddhism. Born a prince, he was devastated upon seeing a sick and dying man. He renounced his life and became a monk. He is an inspiration to millions and Buddhism is the fastest growing spiritual practice globally.

Faith demands no proof.
Patience is the first requisite of spirituality.
Man must never suppress his inner voice even if he stands alone.
More people die of the fear of disease than of disease itself.
Purity is tested only when it is pitted against impurity.

Mahatma Gandhi. Collected from various sources. One such source is Quotable Quotes of Gandhi and Quotes of Gandhi.

Never sacrifice who you are just because someone has a problem with it.

Remind yourself that it's OK not to be perfect.

Believe in yourself.

Speak the truth even if your voice shakes.

Judging a person does not define who they are. It defines who you are.

Always try to see the glass half full.

Remain calm even if it seems hopeless.

Meet new people even if they look different.

Love your friends no matter who they are.

There is always someone who loves you more than you know.

Life's greatest sin—tears in someone's eyes due to you and life's greatest reward/achievement –tears in someone's eyes for you.

Live life according to your needs not according to your wishes. Because needs are fulfilled even of the beggars but wishes would remain fulfilled even of the kings.

Man does not get tired working physically day and night as with anger and worry that tire you out in one second.

In life, nothing is made for itself for example, a river does not drink its own water, a tree does not eat its own fruits, the sun does not give its light for itself, and flowers do not spread their fragrance for themselves. Do you know why? Because living for others is the real life.

(Received on WhatsApp)

QUOTES FROM 'DOVE' CHOCOLATE WRAPPERS
(Messages in Dove chocolates)
Don't stop until you're proud. *Lauren N., Colorado.*
Be the sculptor of your dreams. *Joanne G. California.*
Be fearlessly authentic. *Satiria S., New Jersey.*
Throw kindness around like confetti. *Molly B. Kansas.*
Be with people who make you laugh. *Lucy K., California.*
Hands are to be held. *Carina T., Nevada*
Inhale the future, exhale the past. *Layne R. Ohio.*
After every storm, there's a rainbow no matter how long it takes to show up. *Grace V., Ohio.*

A LESSON OF LIFE FROM OUR HANDS
All fingers are not the same length.
But when they bend, all stand equal.
Life become easy when we bend and adjust to all situations!
(Received on WhatsApp from a Friend)

Select References

"An Inspiration to Countless People, Gish Taught That Life Is Precious" by Rich Tomsu, *The Athens Messenger.* 2010. *Athens News*, August 2010. www.athensnews.com/ohio/article-31680-prominent-local-activist-dies-in-farming-accident.html. Retrieved August 18, 2020.

"Celebrating the American Spirit, the American Profile, Julia Child." The American Profile. *The Athens Messenger,* August 18, 2012.

Child, Julia, Simone Beck and Louisette Bertholle. *Mastering the Art of French Cooking,* published by Knopf, in two volumes, in 1961 and 1970.

"She was Homeless, Now She is Graduating at the Top of Her High School Class," *Athens Messenger.* June 14, 2017.

"Farmer's Son gets 100% scholarship to Cornell," *Times of India*, GLOBAL, Bengaluru, India, July 15, Wednesday, 2020.

"Hugh Jackman's Wife Again Dismisses Those Rumors about her Husband," *The Mercury News*, September 20, 2020. Retrieved September 30, 2020. *Hugh Jackman-thefamouspeople.com*

"Murderer a doc after 14 years of jail," *Times of India*, LIFE section, Sunday, February 16, 2020.

Asma Khan Darjeeling Express.
https://www.greatbritishchefs.com/chefs/asma-khan. Retrieved November 16, 2020

"Top 16 J.K. Rowling Quotes to Inspire Strength Through Adversity," Goalcast.com, May 16, 2017. Retrieved September 25, 2020.

www.jkrowling.com

"Goodall Biography," The Biography Channel (2010). Archived from the original on 10 August 2010. Retrieved October 27, 2020.

Holloway, M., "Profile: Goodall – Gombe's Famous Primate," *Scientific American* 277(4), 42–44, 1997.

Goodall in the Forest Again. *National Geographic:* https://www.nationalgeographic.com/magazine/ April 2003. Retrieved October 2020.

Peterson, Dale. Goodall: The Woman Who Redefined Man. *Mariner Books.* Reprint edition, April 10, 2008.

Ruth Bader Ginsburg Biography. Biography.com Editors. The Biography.com website https://www.biography.com/law-figure/ruth-bader-ginsburg. Access July 13, 2021. Last updated May 7, 2020. Original Published Date April 2, 2014.

Silvey, Anita. Untamed: The Wild Life of Jane Goodall. 2015. *National Geographic Kids.*

https://www.history.com/topics/womens-history/ruth-bader-ginsburg. Retrieved April 04, 2021

https://www.biography.com/law-figure/ruth-bader-ginsburg. Retrieved April 04, 2021

https://www.theguardian.com/us-news/2021/mar/28/justice-justice-thou-shalt-pursue-review-ruth-bader-ginsburg-rbg. Retrieved April 04, 2021

"Ruth Bader Ginsburg: Obituary of the Supreme Court Justice," Published 19 September 2020. https://www.bbc.com/news/world-us-canada-49488374. Retrieved April 04, 2021.

"The Making Of An Icon-Becoming Jane", October 2017, Vol.232 No.4, Official Journal of the National Geographic Society, pp. 38, 43, 49.

"How Ruth Bader Ginsburg's Late Husband, Marty, Helped Her Reach Her Potential." https://www.townandcountrymag.com/society/money-and-power/a26292252/ruth-bader-ginsburg-martin-husband-love-story-rbg/. Published September 19, 2020. Retrieved July 13, 2021.

Britannica.com

Wikipedia.com

Biography.com

List of Contributors

Aparna Akkhial currently lives in Dharwad, in the Indian state of Karnataka, after spending four decades in the U.S.A.

Chandra Akkhial is Emeritus Professor of Economics from Marshall University, West Virginia, U.S.A. He manages a college in Dharwad, in Karnataka, India.

Anita Anand is a development and communications consultant; she writes, paints, bakes, and gardens. She lives in the Delhi area in India.

Ravi Badhwar is a businessman in Columbus, Ohio, U.S.A. He has professional degrees in Catering Technology and Hotel Management from India and U.K. He was the founder of a prominent restaurant, *Yogee*, at Nagpur, India. Later, his brother joined him as co-partner.

Rishi Badhwar is son of Mr. Satinder Badhwar, who was a businessman and a co-partner of the once existed restaurant *Yogee*, at Nagpur, India.

Katie Boehlefeld graduated from Ohio University, Athens, Ohio, U.S.A. in May 2020 with a Bachelor of Science in Integrated Healthcare Studies.

Sandee Bishman retired from Athens County Job and Family Services as an Employment Counselor in 2007. She was an Ohio State Licensed Educational Assistant in Athens County and city school system till she retired.

Alice Bradfield is a retired elementary school teacher and lives with her husband in the foothills of the Adirondack Mountains in Inlet, New York, U.S.A.

Rama Chandrasekar is a homemaker, cook, baker and an active social worker. She lives in Bangalore, Karnataka in India.

Ramesh Chandrasekar is a retired Principal Process Engineer from Abu Dhabi. He and his wife live in Bangalore, Karnataka, India.

Cole Casillas is pursuing an undergraduate degree in Exercise Physiology at Ohio University. He worked as Student Manager at Well Works at Ohio University, Athens, Ohio, U.S.A.

Steve Clusman is Senior Program Director for the YMCA at Chillicothe, Ohio, U.S.A.

Jitendra K. Dewan is a retired Mining Engineer who worked as Manager in many Indian coal companies in the states of Maharashtra, West Bengal and Delhi including the Shah Wallace group. In addition, he also served as Director of the MacNeil & Magor now renamed as Williamson & Magor company located at Kolkata, West Bengal.

Nalini Dewan is a part time social worker based in Gurgaon, Haryana, India.

Satish Dewan is a businessman living in Gurgaon, Haryana, India.

Shreela Goel is a retired Software Engineer who taught undergraduate Biology in the U.S.A.

Sharmila Jayasuriya is Associate Professor of Economics, Ohio University, Athens, Ohio, U.S.A.

Bhanu Kapil presently living in the UK was Visiting Associate Professor, Naropa University, Boulder, Colorado, U.S.A.

Adeel Koshal is a freshman at Vanderbilt University, Nashville, Tennessee, USA.

Manjulika Koshal is Emerita Professor of Management, Ohio University, Athens, Ohio, U.S.A. She also served as the Director of International Administrative Studies at Ohio University for seven years and has over100 publications in scholarly journals.

Rajindar K. Koshal, Emeritus Professor of Economics, Ohio University, Athens, Ohio, U.S.A., was Chair of the department; Director of Development Studies; nominated for the Outstanding Graduate Faculty award and has published in numerous scholarly journals.

Rashmi Luthra, Professor of Public Communication and Culture Studies, University of Michigan-Dearborn, U.S.A.

Rajan Luv retired as General Manager, Hewlett Packard, India and VP, Accenture, India.

Nipun Luv was Senior Dietician at the Malhotra Heart Hospital, New Delhi, India.

Kathleen Marinelli retired as a Math teacher, Athens High School, Athens, Ohio, U.S.A.

RD Malhotra is a retired businessman based in Mumbai, India.

Morgan Glenn-Simons is a graduate student in Clinical Physiology at Ohio University, U.S.A., and a CPA/FA Instructor with the American Heart Association.

Nazareth K. J. retired as the Superintendent of Post Offices in India. He lives with his family at Bangalore, India.

Cindy Parsons is Administrative Specialist, College of Health Sciences and Professions, Ohio University, Athens, Ohio, U.S.A.

Parvati works as a housemaid in India. Her story was narrated to Manjulika Koshal.

Radhika Ramdev is an IT Business Consultant at Deloitte and a foodie, art lover, dog whisperer, yoga practitioner and wannabe hiker, living in Vienna, Virginia, U.S.A.

Priti Rao teaches Economics at The International School, Bangalore, India.

Saroj Sawhney is an architect, based in New Delhi, India.

Kelly Shears is a Radiographer /Mammographer at O'Bleness Hospital, Athens, Ohio, U.S.A.

Kimberly Valentour is retired and served as the Director of the Well Works Program at Ohio University, Athens, Ohio, U.S.A.

Karen Vedder is a retired Counsellor at the Athens High School, Athens, Ohio, U.S.A.

Veha Vig has a B.A. in Biochemistry and Molecular Biology, Boston University, 2019.

About the Author

Dr. Manjulika Koshal is a Emerita Professor at Ohio University, Athens, Ohio. She taught at the School of Business in her specialized areas of Operations Management and International Business. Her teaching experience is rich and varied as she has taught variety of Business students both at the graduate and undergraduate levels in many countries besides thirty years at OU. In addition to teaching, Dr. Koshal held many administrative positions such as Director of a well reputed Graduate Program-International Administrative Studies at OU. Koshal has an impressive record of publications (over 100) in reputed scholarly journals.

Dr. Koshal has also been an active member for the last forty years in American Association of University Women (AAUW) serving in various capacities at her local branch. She also served on the International Fellowships Board of the AAUW at Washington D.C.

A native of India, Koshal made Athens her home 54 years ago after she married her husband Dr. Rajindar K. Koshal, Emeritus Professor of Economics at OU. They have two children and six grandchildren.

In her retirement, Koshal enjoys traveling, gardening, reading, socializing, cooking, and spending time with her happy family.